KOKOSCHKA

Paintings

RICHARD CALVOCORESSI

KOKOSCHKA
Paintings

STUDIO CHARTERHOUSE

EDICIONES POLÍGRAFA, S. A.

The author is grateful to the Tate Gallery for permission
to re-use material first published in the exhibition
catalogue *Oskar Kokoschka 1886-1980* (1986).

Cover illustration:
Adèle Astaire (Detail, fig 55).

Frontispiece:
Kokoschka in the mid-1960s (photo: Horst Tappe).

I.S.B.N.: 84-343-0675-1
Dep. Leg.: B. 7.012 - 1992 (Printed in Spain)

Color separation by Reprocolor Llovet, S. A., Barcelona
Printed and bound by La Polígrafa, S. A.
Parets del Vallès (Barcelona)

Contents

The life of Oskar Kokoschka, who was born in 1886 in a small Austrian town on the Danube, and who died a British subject almost ninety-four years later in French-speaking Switzerland, is surely the most extraordinary in the history of twentieth-century art. Seriously wounded fighting for the Emperor Franz Josef in the First World War, forced to seek refuge from the Nazis in England shortly before the Second, the circumstances of Kokoschka's long, restless and varied life are mirrored to an unusual degree in his art. His pictures speak passionately of the people and places he knew and loved, but also of the artist himself and the ideals which moved him and for which he never ceased to campaign.

A humanist by inclination, with a deep concern for the education of children along visual as much as intellectual or theoretical lines, Kokoschka saw himself as the lone survivor of a great European tradition. At the School of Seeing which he founded in Salzburg in 1953 he attempted in characteristically unconventional fashion to put his ideas into practice. Continual, direct contact with nature was to be the only hope against the threat of an increasingly dehumanized society. At the end of the last war he had written: 'There will be no portrait left of modern man because he has lost face and is turning back towards the jungle.'

As an artist Kokoschka was an individualist, combining elements of Expressionism and Symbolism, with a sense of space and movement inherited from the Baroque, to create images of tremendous vitality and strength. This book celebrates above all his achievements as a portrait painter, perhaps *the* great painter of rootless 'modern man', who brought to the genre a new dimension of psychological richness and complexity. His sweeping visions of cities such as Dresden, London and Prague are also in a sense portraits of a Europe that is once again politically free, if not culturally unified. In his later work Kokoschka explored themes from classical mythology, religion and literature, with results astonishing both for their broad human appeal and for their robust paint handling and luminous colours. This late visionary style was for many years written off by the critics, but a younger generation of artists, students and others has come to appreciate its distinctive character as being fully equal to that of earlier phases in Kokoschka's work.

The past two decades have witnessed a remarkable interest in the cultural life of Vienna at the turn of the century, an interest which is not confined to the German- and English-speaking countries of the western world but which has spread to Italy and even France, culminating in a series of large, interdisciplinary exhibitions over the last few years in Venice, Vienna, Paris and New York. If they were not previously household names, the people who contributed most to the late efflorescence of high culture under the Habsburgs have become so now: Klimt, Kokoschka and Schiele; Wagner, Hoffmann and Loos; Mahler and Schoenberg; Schnitzler and Musil; Freud, Wittgenstein and Kraus.

The picture of 'Vienna 1900' as a homogeneous group of artists and intellectuals, many of them from the liberal Jewish bourgeoisie, battling against a stolid establishment, is largely a myth. Ideas certainly cross-fertilized but not everybody knew one another intimately. Within the avant-garde itself (if such a self-contained entity really existed) there were factions and animosities: that between Loos and Hoffmann, for example, or Kraus and Freud. Different ideals and values co-existed but more often clashed. The early Kokoschka, that is to say up to 1908, is best seen in the context of *Jugendstil*, a florid late-symbolist style similar to *art nouveau*, which made a strong impact on the applied arts and which in painting is associated with the artists of the Vienna Secession. Like so many German and Austrian painters who were to develop in an expressionist direction, Kokoschka's background was in the applied arts. He studied at the School of Applied Arts and in 1907, while still a student, became an associate of the Wiener Werkstätte, the geometrizing design workshops run by the architect Josef Hoffmann. *The Dreaming Youths*, Kokoschka's proto-expressionist illustrated 'fairy-tale', which he dedicated to Klimt, was published by the Werkstätte in 1908. He also designed posters and postcards, and decorated fans for them. But by the summer of 1909, when he graduated from the School, his style and preoccupations had begun to shift fundamentally. Encouraged by the architect Adolf Loos, who took a paternal interest in him, the twenty-three-year-old Kokoschka severed his connection with the Werkstätte and exchanged a moderately secure job in commercial art for the financially uncertain world of the portrait painter. Although his subjects were some of the leading Viennese intellectuals of the day, especially the small circle of writers and musicians around Loos and Kraus, temperamentally he had left 'Vienna 1900' far behind; and within a year had gone to seek his fortune in the more receptive, less provincial climate of Berlin.

The *fin-de-siècle* cult of decadence scarcely affected Kokoschka, although a sense of physical and mental decline is evoked in a number of his early portraits. But the morbid self-consciousness and concern with adolescent eroticism characteristic of the art of Egon Schiele are conspicuously absent. Kokoschka let violence and sexuality emerge in his poems and plays, notably *Murderer Hope of Women* (1909) and its extraordinary line illustrations, with their incisive and aggressive calligraphy. In his paintings he concentrated less on giving a literal record of his

Die träumenden Knaben (The Dreaming Youths),
1908.
Title page and illustrations.

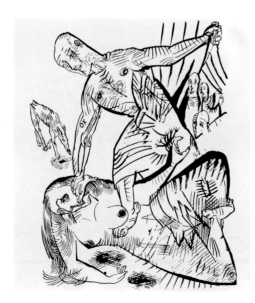

Left.
*Mörder, Hoffnung der Frauen
(Murderer Hope of Women).*
Illustration published in *Der Sturm,*
1910.

Right.
Karl Kraus, drawing by Kokoschka.
Published in *Der Sturm,* 1910.

sitters than on portraying their psychological traits. Factual likeness, though not to be ignored, was subservient to capturing the emotional mood or feel of his subject. In this respect Kokoschka differs substantially from his German Expressionist contemporaries — for instance Kirchner and the artists of *die Brücke* — in whose work the portrait plays a relatively minor role. The *Brücke* insistence on pure saturated colour and spontaneous brushstroke as signifying the primitive or elemental qualities they cultivated has no parallel in Kokoschka's work of this period. Colour is severely muted in the earliest portraits, which give the curious impression of being barely painted at all. As we might expect from someone who began his career as a graphic artist, line is used to great expressive effect.

What was new and shocking about Kokoschka's early portraits was their lack of naturalism. From the start, critics compared their distortions and supposed deformities to caricature — and caricature, or something very like it, is one of the essential tools of the expressionist artist. A number of Kokoschka's subjects were emancipated Jews but by no means all of them had been born in Vienna. From the outlying districts of the Austro-Hungarian Empire in Galicia or Bohemia they converged on Vienna, that melting-pot of different races and cultures. In his portraits Kokoschka suggests their anonymity — they are usually dressed inconspicuously in everyday clothes — vulnerability and rootlessness.

Much has been written of Kokoschka's 'X-ray eyes', his ability to penetrate the minds and even the souls of his models. Kokoschka himself once used the memorable phrase 'a psychological tin-opener'[1] to describe his method of encouraging the sitter to move, talk, read or become absorbed in his or her thoughts, unconscious of the artist's presence, before he would start work. Most of the early portraits are half-lengths, usually stopping just below the hands, on which the artist places heavy emphasis. Fingers are shown clenched or clasped, as in the portraits of Loos (No. 8) and Harta (No. 7); unnaturally bent or distorted (Nos. 6, 15); or long and sensitive as in the majority of female portraits (Nos. 6, 13, 15). Sometimes the hands are outlined or stained in red, an idea developed in portraits from 1911 onwards in subtle passages of flesh and earth tones which evoke the colour and texture of putrefying meat.[2] In the paintings of consumptives done in Switzerland in early 1910 (Nos. 13–16) this blood red is allowed to impregnate the face, giving ominous spots of high colour to an otherwise deathly pale complexion. Facial features may also be delineated in red, suggesting veins or blood vessels (No. 8). The spectator's attention is frequently drawn to the eyes, which are often asymmetrical, with one larger than the other. Their owners occasionally look directly at the spectator but more usually gaze distractedly elsewhere, as if preoccupied with their own inner selves.

Whereas Schiele's figures communicate primarily through body language, Kokoschka's portraits rely on minute inflexions of face and hands for their smouldering psychological charge. Bodies are seldom contorted but remain comparatively inert. In the portrait of Lotte Franzos (No. 6), for example, the subject's body is indicated perfunctorily by a bluish aura drawn around it, while her clothes are almost completely unpainted, leaving visible large areas of ground. Such an insubstantial appearance lends a visionary quality to the image; this is intensified by the blank background which isolates the subject even further and offers no clue to his or her social status or profession. By contrast with their bodies, the sitter's faces and hands seem to twitch and pulsate with life. This can be explained in part by the peculiar manner in which they are painted. Kokoschka would often scratch the wet paint with the sharp end of the brush or possibly with a fingernail, producing lines of varying degrees of thinness which form a complex network of graphic signs at certain crucial points. Sometimes these lines animate the space around the figure, as in the portrait of Joseph de Montesquiou (No. 14), where they perform a decorative function perfectly in keeping with the doll-like appearance of the sickly aristocrat. In Kokoschka's portrait drawings of 1910 — for example that of Karl Kraus — every muscular and nervous tic is exposed on the surface of the skin, joining scars, warts, wrinkles and other external blemishes in a vibrant pattern of marks and dots made with the pen, the equivalent of the brush handle or fingernail.

The paint texture of several early oils is thin and dry, with a rubbed or scraped quality that implies the use of the hands or a cloth. The effect of this flatness and lack of modelling is to convey an eerie sense of immediacy, as if a photographic negative or X-ray of the model has been imprinted on the canvas. A handful of pictures, such as the brightly coloured *Still-life with Pineapple* 1909 (No. 1) and the portraits of Loos, Harta and Father Hirsch (Nos. 8, 7, 2), employ thicker, oilier conglomerations of paint and a more energetic brushstroke, suggesting the influence of Van Gogh, whose work Kokoschka first saw at the international *Kunstschau* in Vienna in the early summer of 1909. Kokoschka's portraits share with Van Gogh's certain obvious characteristics, including a preference for half- or three-quarter-lengths seated against stark backgrounds and depicted full-face or half-turned; and a prominence given to the hands, which are shown either tense or gesticulating (Nos. 19, 21), resting on a table or the back of a chair, folded together (No. 8), or holding an object such as a book (No. 29). But above all it is the humanity and nervous intensity of Van Gogh's images which Kokoschka transposes into his own, idiosyncratic idiom. Whether he also knew Van Gogh's ink drawings, with their hatchings, loops, whorls and other rapid calligraphic strokes, is not recorded; but it seems likely in view of the foregoing.

Van Gogh apart, there seem to have been few influences on Kokoschka's style before 1911. An exception is the nineteenth-century Austrian artist Anton Romako (1832–1889), whose work was collected by Oskar Reichel, the father of the *Boy with Raised Hand* in Kokoschka's portrait of 1910 (private collection). Romako, who eventually committed suicide, was something of an 'outsider', a painter of large-scale historical scenes as well as highly charged portraits of young society women. Their bright staring eyes and rarefied manner may well have influenced Kokoschka. But while Romako's art is in danger of crossing the border into Mannerism, Kokoschka never loses sight of his objective. In his hands the portrait becomes a deposit of human experience, rather like an archaeological site which the artist must excavate (Freud used a similar analogy to describe the psychoanalytical process). Kokoschka's early work is curiously homespun and styleless, a quality that would have appealed to Loos, with his cult of *Sachlichkeit* and dislike of all things arty. One man's honesty, however, may be another's ugliness. There are accounts of Kokoschka's clients refusing to buy, or declining for years to hang, their portraits, on the grounds that they were cruel and 'unlike' themselves, or because they felt they had been made to look thirty years older. Equally, there are stories of a model growing to resemble his or her 'likeness' years afterwards.

It has been remarked that 'the artist is always tempted to invest his models with his own psycho-physical qualities'.[3] Kokoschka was no exception; in later years especially he would project his long upper lip and pugnacious chin on to the faces of his sitters, male or female, so that in extreme cases the finished result is closer to self-portraiture. The notion of empathy is crucial to an understanding of Kokoschka's art: 'I cannot paint everybody. It is only people who are on my antennae ... certain people whom I discovered an affinity with — with one facet of my own being.'[4] This may explain why, in the early portraits, we are rarely given any clues as to the status or interests of the person depicted. Paul Stefan, in the first monograph on Kokoschka published in 1913, laid great stress on the autobiographical element in his work, finding that 'the pictures of this period ... express first of all the artist Kokoschka; they say what he was suffering then'.[5]

A slightly less romantic view was put forward thirty years later by Edith Hoffmann, who recognized a collaborative as well as a therapeutic process in Kokoschka's relationship with his sitters.

Adolf Loos in 1904 (Bildarchiv d. Öst. Nationalbibliothek).

Kokoschka's poster for *Der Sturm*, 1910.

10

Once he had realised what the faces of his friends expressed, he was filled with fear for them; but at the same time was seized by an indomitable urge to relieve his own fears and uncertainties by fixing theirs on his canvas.[6]

Certainly Kokoschka can lay claim to have painted the first existential image of alienated modern man, in which the individual is stripped of mask and pretence — or, to use his own word, 'opened'. Like the sculptor Rubek in Ibsen's *When We Dead Wake* (1899) he could truthfully have said: 'What I turn out aren't just portraits... there's something subtle and equivocal lurking below the surface ...'[7]

During 1911 a change gradually came over Kokoschka's painting, probably as a result of his contacts with the more cosmopolitan art world in Berlin, where he had lived for much of the previous year, helping Herwarth Walden on his expressionist periodical *Der Sturm*. The change is noticeable in works of different type. In portraiture, the subject is rendered with greater plasticity, almost equal attention being paid to the body as to the face and hands. Gone are the etiolated, semi-transparent forms of 1909–10, to be replaced by emphatically modelled volumes and a more mature sense of the possibilities of colour and brushwork. New structural concerns are evident in the series of paintings on biblical themes (e.g. No. 23), in which the figures are integrated with their environment by a dense all-over faceting. This softening of outline, which can likewise be seen in the portrait of Egon Wellesz (No. 19), is a striking departure from Kokoschka's earlier employment of a sharp contour to define physical mass. It recalls Cubism, as, too, does the general opacity of the 1911 pictures. In 1912, however, Kokoschka broke through to a sparkling translucency in paintings such as *Alpine Landscape, Mürren* (No. 24) and the portrait of Alma Mahler (No. 26). The pastel colours, particularly pink, blue, green and yellow, and the fragmented, crystalline structure of these works suggest the influence of a cubist offshoot such as Robert Delaunay.

Delaunay's work would have been familiar to Kokoschka. Four of his pictures were included in the *Blaue Reiter* exhibitions which toured Germany in the winter of 1911–12 and which Herwarth Walden incorporated in his first *Sturm* exhibition (in which Kokoschka was represented) at Berlin in March 1912. Walden showed Delaunay again in the second *Sturm* exhibition in April. Apart from his connection with Walden, Kokoschka had reasonably good relations with the *Blaue Reiter* through his friendship with Schoenberg. But there is a second, literary source which may conceivably account for Kokoschka's jewel-like style of 1912: the utopian architectural theories of Paul Scheerbart. Scheerbart was closely involved with *Der Sturm*; in 1910 Kokoschka painted his portrait (No. 18) and also drew him for the magazine. Scheerbart's crystalline vision, which he had been refining since the 1890s, was finally published in *Der Sturm* in 1914. In it he speaks of a spiritual need to 'transform our architecture'.

... this will be possible only if we remove the enclosed quality from the spaces within which we live. This can be done only through the introduction of glass architecture that lets the sunlight and the light of the moon and stars into our rooms not merely through a few windows, but simultaneously through the greatest possible number of walls that are made entirely of glass-coloured glass.[8]

Finally, it is worth noting that Kokoschka, according to Edith Hoffmann, was experimenting with a prism at this time.[9]

Kokoschka's new-founded painterliness was also in part a result of his engagement with the older masters, to begin with El Greco, who was then being rediscovered in Germany. The figures in Kokoschka's small religious pictures probably derive from El Greco, their pale, drawn faces, elongated bodies and stylized hand gestures evoking a mystical dimension in keeping with the subject matter. In his portraits, with their frontality, austerity and, not least, dark, almost black backgrounds, Kokoschka reveals even more clearly his debt to El Greco, whom many years later he would recognize as 'an expressionist painter'.[10]

He was also drawn to the heightened colours and dramatic illusionism of Franz Anton Maulbertsch (1724–96), the leading Austrian master of late Baroque, whose breathtaking ceiling frescoes in the Piaristenkirche in Vienna had made such a profound impression on him as a boy. In later years a baroque sense of space and movement became a hallmark of Kokoschka's style, as in *The Prometheus Saga* triptych of 1950 (No. 92), also a ceiling painting, where he may have been consciously recalling Maulbertsch. But his strongest admiration at this time was reserved for the Venetians, especially Titian and Tintoretto, whose works he saw on a visit to Venice with Alma Mahler in March 1913. The great symbolic compositions of 1913–15, in which Kokoschka either celebrates his love for Alma Mahler, reflects on its problems, or predicts the end of the relationship (Nos. 25, 28, 30, 31, 32), demonstrate a freer technique and an awareness of light as a means of enlivening surface and denoting depth. Paint is generally creamier and applied in broad, fluid strokes. Colour, though often restricted to a sombre range of blue and green or brown and grey tones, is rich and sensuous, while forms are highlighted with bold touches of white, sometimes flecked with red, causing the image to quiver

Alma Mahler (Bildarchiv d. Öst. Nationalbibliothek).

Kokoschka in the uniform of a dragoon in the Austro-Hungarian army, 1915 (Kokoschka archive, Villeneuve).

Kokoschka on the Galician front, 1915 (Kokoschka archive, Pöchlarn).

before our eyes. The predominant effect is one of restless, dynamic movement.

In *Two Nudes* (No. 28), the lovers clutch each other in a kind of heavenly dance; both are shown naked and vulnerable. One cannot imagine that this intimate expression of love was ever intended for public scrutiny. Kokoschka associated Alma Mahler with the 'Liebestod' from *Tristan*, which she had sung to him, accompanying herself on the piano, at their first meeting. (It is worth noting that an earlier title for *The Tempest* was *Tristan and Isolde*.) *The Tempest*, *Still-life with Putto and Rabbit* and *Knight Errant*, despite their iconographic complexity, are all self-allegories of haunting power: not until the Second World War would Kokoschka be roused to produce works of equal emotional intensity.

In January 1915, five months after the outbreak of war, Kokoschka volunteered for a cavalry regiment in the Austro-Hungarian army. Eight months later he was badly injured in the head and the lung during a skirmish with Russians on the eastern front. At the end of October he was brought back to Vienna, where he remained in hospital until February 1916 and convalesced for a further three months. In July Kokoschka was posted south to the Italian front to serve as an officer responsible for looking after war artists and journalists. In late August he developed shell-shock and was transferred once again to a military hospital in Vienna. A week later he was released and given extended sick leave by the army.

By the end of the year, after a brief stay in Berlin, Kokoschka had been admitted to a sanatorium in the wooded Weisser Hirsch district of Dresden. Here, at a nearby inn, he met a handful of pacifists, most of them expressionist actors, playwrights or poets, who became his companions and whom he used as models in two symbolic group portraits, *The Exiles* 1916–17 and *The Friends* (No. 35). Other paintings of this period, such as *Lovers with Cat* (No. 34), demonstrate a feverishness in execution which may reflect the artist's precarious state of health. Scarred both physically and psychologically by his wartime experiences, Kokoschka was further depressed by the breakup of his affair with Alma Mahler. The trend towards greater naturalism discernible in the portraits of 1911–14 is now reversed. Paint is worked into a thick impasto by means of writhing, organic brushstrokes, so that at certain points the forms appear to loosen and even dissolve altogether.

Lovers with Cat is one of a handful of major oils, including *The Tempest* (No. 30) and *Woman in Blue* (No. 38), for which there are preliminary drawings in pencil or ink. Otherwise Kokoschka rarely made preparatory sketches, with the exception of the occasional more

The Exiles, 1916–17, oil on canvas, 37⅜ × 57½ in. (95 × 146 cm), Bayerische Staatsgemäldesammlungen, Munich.

ambitious or formal portrait, such as those of Masaryk (No. 67), Maisky (No. 83), and Kathleen, Countess of Drogheda (No. 85), for which detailed studies exist. The early portraits, on the other hand, were all painted direct from the sitter.

If the paintings of 1917–19 suggest a degree of formal incoherence, those of 1920 onwards, beginning with *The Power of Music* (No. 37), seem by comparison more compact and resolved. In terms of colour they relate to German Expressionism, for instance Nolde and some of the artists of the *Brücke,* whose work Kokoschka knew from his association with Herwarth Walden in Berlin before the war. The composition is now organised in irregularly shaped smears and patches of pure unmixed colour — usually green and the primaries, especially red — which are not divided by contour lines but which abut one another directly. The effect is of a dazzling radiance similar to stained glass. Kokoschka himself was the first to recognize the monumental or environmental possibilities of his new language of colour. He had in fact been commissioned by the architect Max Berg to paint frescoes for a crematorium at Breslau shortly before the First World War; and, although the project was never realized, he remained interested in the problems of creating a cycle of large-scale images intended to be seen from a distance.[11]

The Power of Music, Mother and Child (No. 42) and *The Slave Girl* (No. 47) are double-figure compositions with sensual and violent overtones, suggesting that pathos and brooding introspection were still important elements in Kokoschka's work. The series of Dresden townscapes, however (e.g. Nos. 40, 44, 45, 46), strikes a lighter, more optimistic note. In the summer of 1919 Kokoschka was appointed to a professorship at the Dresden Academy, a job he had coveted ever since arriving in the city over two years previously. He moved into his studio in the academy, which overlooked the Elbe, in the autumn, and from its balcony painted the first of several views across the wide river with its elegant bridges. The baroque houses and spires huddled together on the opposite bank are translated by Kokoschka into a jostling patchwork of small planes and strips of colour. In one picture of the series, *Dresden, the Elbe Bridges (with figure from behind)* (No. 46), the silhouette of his own head and shoulders dominates the foreground, turned away from the spectator in contemplation of the scene, while a yellow tram crosses the nearest bridge beneath which a barge floats silently by. Such details look forward to those atmospheric panoramas in which he would brilliantly convey the very essence of London, Prague and other centres of European civilization which meant so much to him.

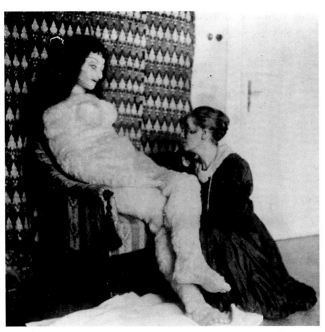

Puppet-maker Hermine Moos with the life-size doll made for Kokoschka, 1919 (Kokoschka archive, Villeneuve).

Self-portrait with Doll (No. 39), executed in the broad flat brushstrokes typical of this period, brings us to the strange episode of the life-size doll or puppet which Kokoschka commissioned in the image of Alma Mahler. Every detail of its construction, articulation and external appearance, down to the colour of the hair and soft texture of the 'skin', was closely supervised by the artist, who corresponded at length with the puppet-maker Hermine Moos between August 1918 and February 1919, when the creature was ready to be dispatched to its owner. Kokoschka's instructions were illustrated with anatomical drawings and diagrams; a selection of his letters was later published in an anthology under the title *The Fetish* (1926). Stories of what the disillusioned Kokoschka did or did not do with his 'beloved' once it had arrived — some true, others wildly exaggerated — have been repeated ever since. What is certain is that he made over twenty drawings of the doll and used it as a model for the painting *Woman in Blue* (which, like *The Power of Music*, is built up of slabs of contrasting pigment).

There has been much speculation about Kokoschka's motives in ordering the doll. The artists's own version was that, after his first-hand experience of brutality and destruction, he could no longer tolerate humanity — a reaction to the war not uncommon among German artists if we consider the nervous breakdowns suffered by Max Beckmann and Ernst Ludwig Kirchner. But in Kokoschka's case the phobia extended only to man: throughout his life he preferred and sought out the company of women, whom he regarded as his protectors. A more likely theory is that the artist was determined to live up to the image of *der tolle Kokoschka,* 'crazy Kokoschka', a nickname conferred upon him in Dresden in 1918 but one which echoed the bewildered and sometimes hostile comments of the Viennese nearly a decade earlier. Whether genuine mental imbalance was also involved, we are not in a position to judge. Certainly by the time the artist left Dresden and set off on his travels in the summer of 1923, Kokoschka the nihilist (he had briefly been taken up by the Zurich Dadaists in 1917) was a figure of the past.

Given the disintegrating political and economic situation in Weimar Germany, it is not surprising that Kokoschka should have wished to leave Dresden. Furthermore, having gained recognition in Germany, his work was slowly becoming known internationally, and he was eager to consolidate his position. At the 1922 Venice Biennale he shared the German pavilion on an equal basis with the three giants of so-called German Impressionism, Liebermann, Slevogt and Corinth. Throughout the next decade exhibitions of his work occurred with increasing regularity, not only in the principal German cities but also in Zurich, Amsterdam, London and Paris.

A summary of Kokoschka's movements between August 1923, when he left Dresden, and September 1930, when he settled in Paris, gives some idea of his astonishing energy and intense curiosity for new sights. During those seven years — that is, between the ages of thirty-seven and forty-four — he visited eleven different European countries (including Ireland and Scotland) and explored much of North Africa and the Middle East. His travels began in earnest in February 1925, when his agent, the famous Berlin art dealer Paul Cassirer, agreed to subsidize his trips on a generous scale in exchange for a regular supply of landscapes. Kokoschka was accompanied on these journeys by Jakob Goldschmidt, an associate of Cassirer's, who owned a gallery at Frankfurt. Goldschmidt's job was to take care of the hotel and travelling arrangements, make sure the artist had canvas, easel and paints, and dispatch the finished pictures to Berlin. After Cassirer's death in early 1926 Goldschmidt's place was taken by the more sympathetic Helmut Lütjens, who ran the Amsterdam branch of Cassirer's. Lütjens was Kokoschka's travelling companion on his visits to Italy, Switzerland and France in 1927, and to North Africa and Ireland in 1928, although he would return periodically to Amsterdam, leaving Kokoschka, who relied on him, usually feeling lonely. An art historian who specialized in drawings, Lütjens treated his charge with tact and

Kokoschka in North Africa, 1928
(Kokoschka archive, Villeneuve).

understanding, normally going on ahead of Kokoschka to select views for him to paint.

The dating of the so-called 'travel pictures' has been made easier by the survival of a succession of illustrated post-cards which Kokoschka sent to his family in Vienna and to other friends, sometimes at the rate of two or three a week. On the back of these cards he would invariably give a brief account of his progress, noting the start or completion of a painting, the state of the weather, his future plans and so on. In the case of the three Scottish landscapes of summer 1929, he sent back picture post-cards showing the actual motif of each: whether the purchase of a particularly striking or unusual photograph inspired him to go and search out the original must remain a matter for conjecture. On this occasion there was no Lütjens to help him choose the most picturesque spots, although Walter Feilchenfeldt, one of Cassirer's successors in Berlin, brought Kokoschka to the north of Scotland and stayed with him there for a few days.

Whenever he could, Kokoschka preferred to look down on his motif from a high viewpoint, climbing to the top of a hill or the tenth floor of a building in order to achieve maximum breadth and distance. He also adopted the technique of painting the same picture from two different standpoints, so that, as he later recalled, 'I doubled the width of my visual field'[12], reshaping the landscape to conform to his own vision of the place. In his cityscapes Kokoschka reveals most clearly his debt to the Baroque. The entire canvas is activated; it teems with incident and life. Straight lines become curves, so that buildings seem to 'grow, move and breathe'.[13] Classical, single vanishing-point perspective is discarded in favour of baroque illusionistic space. Kokoschka himself said he 'wanted to interest the onlooker like a book ... He ought to discover new little things here and there. His eyes ought to be led on a promenade through the picture'.[14]

In these paintings of the twenties Kokoschka fully lived up to the promise he had already shown as a landscape artist in *'Les Dents du Midi'* of 1910 (No. 12), which so convincingly reproduces the invigorating sight of an ethereal Alpine landscape under snow. In that work the sun is shown breaking through mist or cloud, a typically baroque effect which Kokoschka repeated in the twenties and which he continued to use up until the last landscapes of the 1960s, though his manner of suggesting light became more summary, almost ideographic. But the similarities with the earlier picture end there. To suit his new habit of painting in the open air or from hotel balconies, Kokoschka evolved a style radically different even from the works of the immediately preceding Dresden phase. In the latter, the spectator is made conscious of paint as *material,* as if it were a substance like clay which the artist has worried and moulded into thick slabs; colour breaks free from its descriptive function and assumes an autonomous role.

Instead of oil paint being applied straight from the tube, however, it is now diluted with turpentine, allowing a swifter execution and resulting in a thinner, transparent surface closer to watercolour. Line reappears in Kokoschka's painting, though in an informal, sketchy manner which bears no relation to the hard contours and incisions of the early portraits: drawing and colour are now indistinguishable. There is nevertheless nothing hesitant about the brush marks, which are rapidly made and numerous. Every variegated touch contributes an essential note to the description of a scene in all its detail, and has its place in the composition. Objects such as buildings are foreshortened (but never gratuitously distorted), the more to give an illusion of deep space. The longest Kokoschka took to complete a landscape was about two weeks; the shortest, according to Edith Hoffmann, 'a day or two'.[15] In northern Europe he was frequently held up by bad weather — fog in London, pelting rain in Inverness-shire. He therefore needed to codify his myriad impressions as quickly as possible, before the light changed and conditions worsened. The scudding March skies of the two 1926 Thames views (Nos. 51, 53) are among the grandest he ever painted; while in *Lyon* (No. 58), with its seagulls dipping and soaring overhead, we can almost feel the artist's presence, wrapped in a thick overcoat against the chilly December gusts.

Water clearly fascinated Kokoschka, nowhere more so than when the heart of a big city was bisected by a broad, mysterious river. In his autobiography he leaves us in no doubt that what attracted him to London was the Thames, 'that artery of life flowing from century to century'.[16] His excitement at seeing the metropolis for the first time is conveyed in the following postcard to his mother, written on 15 July 1925.

> Within my first hour of reaching London I immediately found the right place to paint from. On the 10th floor of a building by the Thames. Below me the whole of the river and a city 10 times the size of Vienna.[17]

Towards the end of his ten-day stay he confided to a friend that

> The country made a very strong impression on me, because it was my first experience of an Anglo-Saxon nation and I needed several days to get over my very great astonishment. And also because in the near future I shall be relying on these people and want to be accepted by them. I took it much more seriously than Paris, Madrid or Rome, etc.[18]

The next year Kokoschka decided to return for longer, postponing plans to visit Egypt and Palestine. He intended to 'paint the 15–20 pictures I want to get done this year in England, on the coast, and in Scotland and Ireland'.[19] In the event he appears to have spent most of his time, from March to September 1926, in London; he did not travel to Ireland until 1928, and it was the summer of 1929 before he finally reached the Highlands of Scotland.

In addition to the Thames views, which were painted from the eighth floor of the Savoy Hotel, Kokoschka completed some half-dozen pictures during his stay in London, including a portrait of the dancer Adèle Astaire (No. 55) and three animal subjects: the exotic *Mandrill* (No. 56) and *Tigon* (No. 57), both painted at Regent's Park Zoo, and a family of deer surprised in Richmond Park. Shortly after arriving he wrote a letter to his mother which expresses the touching mixture of awe and affection with which he regarded the English.

> ...here I am living on the 8th floor of the smartest hotel in Europe. You can imagine how inhibited I feel; I daren't even breathe,... Millions of people, hundreds of thousands of cars, my English useless, my memory gone to pot, my hearing defective; in other words, I feel like a stone on the street. I have to live this high up because from here I can paint the broadest vista of the Thames!
> ...I feel as apprehensive as a schoolboy, even though I'm so long in the tooth ... We in Vienna are like negroes or savages by comparison with the real world of the English.[20]

By the spring of 1927 Kokoschka's financial situation had improved sufficiently for him to consider moving to England with his mother and younger brother, who were both dependent on him.[21] However, the idea, if it was ever very practicable, came to nothing. The following year the Leicester Galleries in London held a one-man exhibition of thirty-four paintings, his first ever in Britain. The catalogue carried a brief introduction by P. G. Konody, who took trouble to distinguish Kokoschka from the German Expressionists (who, he thought, were unlikely ever to be collected by the English) and gave a perceptive appraisal of the artist's most recent work. In spite of Konody's enthusiasm, however, the exhibition was not a success. T. W. Earp in *The New Statesman* described it as 'a salad compounded to a clever recipe ... energy and virtuosity ... singularly lacking in significance', although he did make an allowance for Kokoschka as a 'good, "straight" landscape' painter.[22] Kokoschka, who came to London for the opening, did not return to the city for another ten years, and then in very different circumstances.

Several commentators have attributed Kokoschka's years of *Wanderschaft* to his desire to create a modern version of the *Orbis Pictus,* a book which had made a lasting impact on him as a child.[23] In a long footnote to Edith Hoffmann's monograph, written during the dark days of the Second World War but not published until 1947, Kokoschka reaffirmed his belief in the importance of this illustrated encyclopaedia and the ideas of its author — the seventeenth-century Moravian theologian, pacifist and pedagogue Jan Amos Comenius (or Komensky) — which seemed to him especially relevant now that the whole world was plunged into violent conflict.

> It pictured men of all nations as belonging to one family differing only in colour, language, religion, in their dwellings, habits, activities and sciences, and showed that these divisions were due to geography and climate.... Words inscribed beneath the pictures in several living and dead languages, made it easy to learn the meaning when you could see the things and knew them to be true.[24]

But there were other, more personal reasons behind Kokoschka's conscious decision to broaden his horizons, which orginate in the crisis he suffered during the First World War. In an interview with the critic Andrew Forge in 1962, he recalled his feelings at that traumatic moment in his life.

> And then I thought ... if I ever come out of this rat-existence alive, I will paint landscapes, because I have seen so little of the world, so I want to see everywhere, I want to go everywhere where the roots of my culture, of my civilization, are which lead back to the Greek, the Latin: I must see all that.[25]

Despite his preoccupation with landscape in the twenties, Kokoschka did not neglect portraiture, but continued to produce good work. While staying with his family in Vienna he took the opportunity to paint his old friends Arnold Schoenberg (No. 49), in 1924, and Karl Kraus (No. 52) in 1925. Nothing is allowed to detract in either portrait from the image of the sensitive artist concentrating on his particular task — Schoenberg playing the cello, Kraus fingering a book with one hand and gesturing with the other, as if reciting. Fine examples of expressionist portraiture though they undoubtedly are, they nevertheless typify the same systematic, less intuitive approach to subject matter that characterizes Kokoschka's townscapes and landscapes. This becomes more evident later in the decade, with the portraits of the Marabout of Temacine (No. 60) and Marczell von Nemeš (No. 59), in each of which the figure is drawn in greater volume and depth than hitherto and occupies more of the canvas. If the degree of paraphrase is minimal in comparison with the 'psychological' portraits of 1909–11, it is made up for by the massiveness of the subject, whose physical presence seems all the more palpably real. As if to balance this naturalistic treatment of the human figure, Kokoschka introduces a narrative element, for example in the portrait of Adèle Astaire (No. 55), where background objects or symbols allude to the interests and profession, and by im-

Karl Kraus (Bildarchiv d. Öst. Nationalbibliothek).

plication the personality, of the sitter. Over the next twenty years Kokoschka would increasingly resort to this convention, sometimes including a complete scene in the background.

Adèle Astaire is portrayed with her dog, whose features wittily echo those of its mistress. Kokoschka's insight into animal character is demonstrated by the magnificent paintings of a mandrill and a tigon mentioned above. Both were hung in his exhibition, significantly titled *Portraits by Oskar Kokoschka: Humans and Animals,* held at Cassirer's in February 1927, alongside the portraits of Kraus, Nancy Cunard (No. 50) and Adèle Astaire. Concerning the mandrill Kokoschka later wrote: 'As I painted him, I saw: this is a wild, isolated fellow, almost a mirror image of myself who wants to be alone.'[26]

For the first nine months of 1931 Kokoschka lived in Paris, the reputation of which as the European capital of fine art he regarded with suspicion, if not disdain. Years later at Salzburg he would warn his students of the corrupting influence of the 'beauty industry', as he dubbed the School of Paris.[27] In March 1931, however, Paris did Kokoschka the peculiar honour of a one-man exhibition at the Galeries Georges Petit, which was actually a reduced version of his retrospective held at Mannheim earlier in the year. It was surprisingly well received, and for a while it must have looked to Kokoschka that he was poised on the brink of international acclaim. Simultaneously with the exhibition at Petit's, the Museum of Modern Art in New York organized a large survey of *German Painting and Sculpture,* in which Kokoschka was repre-

Kokoschka in his Paris studio, 1931 (photo: Brassaï).

sented by four oils, including *Woman with Parrot* (No. 33) and *Girl with Doll* (No. 43).

In Paris Kokoschka rented a studio above the British painter Augustus John, who later did much to help Austrian and German artists find refuge from the Nazis in England.[28] In the summer of 1931 Kokoschka took over the house and studio of his friend the painter Jules Pascin, who had committed suicide. He also met and was photographed by Brassaï. But in September 1931, his contract with Cassirer's having collapsed some months previously, he was forced for financial reasons to return once more to Vienna. He spent a further year in Paris, from March 1932 to May 1933, during which time he painted a handful of works. It was in Vienna, however, that his art discovered a new sense of purpose, which grew stronger as the decade progressed inexorably towards its conclusion.

In 1920 Kokoschka had managed to buy his parents a villa in the Liebhartstal, a pleasant district on the western outskirts of Vienna consisting of mainly wooden houses, surrounded by gardens, orchards and avenues of chestnut trees. It was to this peaceful environment that Kokoschka withdrew in the autumn of 1931, in time for his mother's seventieth birthday (his father had died in 1923). Refreshed and stimulated by his surroundings, he made friends with a fifteen-year-old girl, the daughter of a neighbour, who agreed to pose for him. In all, some twenty drawings and half dozen paintings of Trudl exist, showing her in a variety of roles and moods (e.g. Nos. 64, 65). In their heavy, rounded forms and air of classical repose, these pictures are the direct antithesis of the portraits of neurotic-looking individuals whose psyches he had probed, with an astonishing indifference to matters of technical skill, over twenty years earlier.

Chance played its part in turning Kokoschka's attention again to questions of content. Shortly after his arrival he was commissioned by the socialist council of 'Red Vienna' to paint a picture for a prominent place in the Town Hall. For a suitable theme he looked no further than his immediate neighbourhood. The Liebhartstal lies between two hills, the Galitzinberg and the Wilhelminenberg. Five minutes walk uphill from the Kokoschkas' house stood Schloß Wilhelminenberg, a former Habsburg palace which had been acquired cheaply by the authorities in 1927 and converted into a children's home. Kokoschka was moved and encouraged by this and other social services provided by the municipality during the harsh economic years of the First Republic. As he could hear and see the children from his second-floor studio window playing in the palace grounds, he decided to paint them.

Vienna, View from the Wilhelminenberg (No. 63), for which Kokoschka made several preparatory pencil sketches from different viewpoints, is a townscape with a difference. Although the background affords a panoramic view of the whole city, in which distant landmarks such as the spire of the nineteenth-century Gothic *Rathaus* are clearly visible, the focus of the composition rests in the foreground activity. In the park beneath the palace little knots and clusters of children are shown playing specific games. Kokoschka based this idea on a famous painting by Brueghel, *Children's Games*, in the Kunsthistorisches Museum. Somehow he must have connected it in his mind with Comenius and the latter's ideal (as Kokoschka himself later put it) of 'the education of people to reason on the basis of using their five senses',[29] since each of the children's games in the picture — blind man's buff, ring-a-ring-a-roses and so on — involves the use of a different sense. Kokoschka argued that received opinion, second-hand knowledge, hearsay, or whatever we like to call it, was largely responsible for society's ills. To support his case he quoted St. Thomas Aquinas: 'the senses are a kind of reason. Taste, touch and smell, hearing and seeing, are not merely a means to sensation, enjoyable or otherwise, but they are also a means to knowledge — and are, indeed, your only actual means to knowledge...'[30] This may explain why he later called his summer school at Salzburg (1953–63) the 'School of Seeing'. No ordinary painting academy, its courses were designed to free students from preconceptions and second-hand ideas — to open their eyes. When drawing figures in motion — a practice Kokoschka had introduced as early as 1912 to the School of Applied Arts in Vienna, where he taught a life class — the students at Salzburg were encouraged to capture the living, transitory moment or impression rather than produce a detailed, academic study of a nude model.

Wilhelminenberg, then, is a symbolic painting. Given the high value Kokoschka attached to the ideal of visual and constructive education independent of militaristic or nationalistic concerns, it is not difficult to understand why he later referred to it as his 'first picture with a political meaning'.[31]

Kokoschka's mother died in July 1934. Two months later, finding the political developments in Austria intolerable and disappointed by the lack of portrait commissions, he left for Prague. The four years he spent there were, in terms of his art, productive ones, but they were spoiled by the deteriorating international situation, uncertainty over his own future, financial worries and ill health. An outspoken opponent of Nazi cultural and educational policies, Kokoschka had published in a German newspaper an open letter in support of Max Liebermann after the latter, on account of his Jewish blood, was forced to resign as President of the Prussian Academy in May 1933. Furthermore, Kokoschka's pictures were beginning to be confiscated by the Nazis from German museums as examples of 'cultural Bolshevism'. But however grim the events in Germany, he was relieved to be away from the 'oppressive little world' of Vienna.[32] Even when the city finally got round to giving him a retrospective in 1937 he refused to go back for it, and after the *Anschluß* of March 1938 he realized that to return to Vienna would mean denunciation and imprisonment. At least in Prague there was freedom of speech and a cosmopolitan atmosphere which he found sympathetic. He respected the people and their civilized traditions; and he fell in love with the city, which he painted more times than any other.

In the summer of 1935 Kokoschka took as his studio a turret in the roof of a tall nineteenth-century building on the banks of the River Moldau, which gave him a spectacular view of the medieval Charles Bridge and the Hradschin castle on its hill opposite. It was in Prague that Kokoschka met Olda Palkovská, a young law student who was soon sharing his eccentric life and who later proved indispensable in helping the artist leave Czechoslovakia.

The two masterpieces of Kokoschka's Prague period, the first of which can be read as a political testimony, are the portrait of Thomas G. Masaryk (No. 67) and the ironically titled *Self-portrait of a "Degenerate Artist"* (No. 71). The permission to paint the first President of

Kokoschka on his studio balcony overlooking the River Moldau and Charles Bridge, Prague, 1935 or 1936 (Kokoschka archive, Villeneuve).

Thomas G. Masaryk, President of Czechoslovakia, in 1936 (BBC Hulton Picture Library).

the Czechoslovak Republic may have arrived before Kokoschka left Vienna. He instinctively warmed to this eighty-five-year-old who, he later wrote, 'will always stand as a symbol of democratic freedom'.[33] Their conversations ranged widely but tended to concentrate on Masaryk's humane educational policies, which reinforced Kokoschka's own half-formulated ideas. Their mutual admiration for Comenius was a frequent topic of discussion. In the portrait, Kokoschka explicitly links Masaryk with Comenius, who is shown by the President's side holding up a tract, his *Via Lucis*, on which are illustrated the five sensory organs. Three months after starting work on the portrait Kokoschka said in an interview:

> ... According to Comenius it is easier to teach by means of pictures than by means of words; and so a modern, symbolic portrait like this should serve to be instructive ... Neither cape nor crown, neither sceptre nor sword, denote this President's status ... I want to make it a historical picture; a picture that can be shown in schools, to teach the children that patriotic tasks, as well as personal duties are united in humanism.[34]

The self-portrait, even more than the portrait of Masaryk, announces the move to a more monumental style first intimated in Kokoschka's paintings of the mid-twenties but not fully evolved until the *Trudl* series. It is a work of great plasticity and psychological depth. Shortly after starting work on the painting, Kokoschka heard the news from Germany that eight of his pictures had been included in the Nazis' notorious exhibition of *Degenerate 'Art'* at Munich. His immediate response was to alter the position of his arms so that they crossed in an attitude of defiance. The inclusion of a running figure as well as a stag in the background is a clear allusion to flight or pursuit — the artist as hunted man. One can imagine Kokoschka's feelings when he learned that the *Degenerate 'Art'* exhibition was to be toured round Germany like a freak-show, ending up in Vienna in the autumn of 1938. At the end of November 1937 he wrote to his future biographer Edith Hoffmann in London, mentioning

> A New Self-portrait ... suggestive and very good ... it could be called 'Self-Portrait of a Pilloried Artist'. But it looks as if I'll have the last laugh at those fools' expense.[35]

Finally, not the least remarkable aspect of this searching self-portrait is Kokoschka's brushwork, the superficial untidiness and spontaneity of which conceals a deft, assured touch which unites all the disparate elements of form, colour and tone into a resonant whole.

On 18th October 1938, less than three weeks after the Munich agreement which effectively delivered Czechoslovakia into Nazi hands, Kokoschka and Olda Palkovská managed to fly to London. Kokoschka entered the country on a Czech passport, Masaryk having helped him to apply for Czech citizenship in 1935 — a step which was late to prove beneficial to the artist. In the panic of summer 1940, after the fall of France, thousands of German and Austrian refugees were classified by Parliament as 'enemy aliens' and interned. Czechs, on the other hand, were deemed to be 'friendly aliens', with a government-in-exile in London headed by Edvard Beneš; and although their movements about Britain were restricted, they were otherwise more or less left in peace. Kokoschka was thus in a good position to campaign for the release of his anti-Nazi and Jewish friends, including artists, from internment camps, and indeed for the repeal of the enemy alien law altogether. This was in line with the policies of the Free Austrian Movement and the Free German League of Culture, the main anti-Nazi refugee organizations in which he took an active part. In December 1941 Kokoschka called for an end to the 'scandal' of internment, which he denounced as 'the skeleton in the wardrobe of democracy',[36] and for internees to be allowed to contribute to the war effort, especially since the Soviet Union had now been forced to join the fight against Hitler and the opening of a Second Front seemed a possibility.

Despite the setback of 1928, when his one-man exhibition at the Leicester Galleries attracted disappointing notices, Kokoschka's attitude towards England had remained positive. 'I like the English so much, as if they were my relatives', he wrote to Anna Kallin from Prague in February 1936.[37]

His admiration, however, was soon tempered by understandable feelings of bitterness at the politics of appeasement and of mounting tension as war approached. Apart from anxiety about his own and Olda's personal future, he still had close relatives in Vienna and Prague (as did she). During the first nine months of the war he became increasingly depressed by what he identified as a growing hostility to foreign refugees, encouraged by a xenophobic English press, among people he had always associated with high standards of toleration. Nevertheless, as he wrote to Philip Moysey, his first English 'pupil', in the early summer of 1940, he was 'still optimistic as an artist to believe more in the good in man and not in the evil'.[38] Nor would he allow himself to feel an exile in Britain, or indeed in any country that was still free and part of European civilization. He was, after all, used to travelling light, and neither he nor Olda were sentimentally attached to particular countries or cities.

Readers of *The Spectator* in March 1936, shortly after Kokoschka's fiftieth birthday, would have found him praised as 'the most important German painter since the death of Liebermann'[39] — a judgement with which few

Polperro harbour.

Kokoschka with *Loreley*, London, *c.* 1942 (photo: Erich Auerbach).

English critics felt able to concur when nineteen of Kokoschka's works, including the *Self-portrait of a "Degenerate Artist"* and *Herwarth Walden*, were shown in the exhibition *20th century German Art* two years later at the New Burlington Galleries in London. Kokoschka himself had reservations about this exhibition, which was conceived as a gesture of moral, and, it was to be hoped, financial support for artists who were being ostracized by Hitler's barbarous cultural policies. To many people, however, it only confirmed their prejudice against German art. Even Liebermann was compared unfavourably to the French Impressionists.

A few weeks before the outbreak of war Kokoschka and Olda Palkovská left London, which was becoming too expensive for them, and went to live in the picturesque fishing village of Polperro on the southern coast of Cornwall, where the Austrian sculptor Uli Nimptsch and his family had settled. In a letter to the painter Hilde Goldschmidt Kokoschka described Polperro as a 'beautiful, healthy place ... much lovelier than a cosy little Italian port because so much more real' (*viel echter*).[40] His opinion was evidently not shared by the writer Rayner Heppenstall, who recounts a visit to Kokoschka in his autobiographical novel *Saturnine* (1943), the dustjacket of which Kokoschka illustrated.

> Never had I seen a place so female, so closely shut in as this inhabited cleft between two plump hills, opening out at the front into a harbour over which one felt that hands were crossed in modesty. As a place to inhabit in the ordinary way, it was horrible.
> I bore left along the crease between the right buttock and thigh, a little above the level at which this mighty, inverted limb plunges into the water.[41]

However ironical, the author succeeds in this extract in catching the intrinsically dramatic quality of the Polperro landscape, which alters with every step, revealing a succession of new shapes and vistas, both natural and man-made but all worn by centuries of fierce storms. Some of Kokoschka's finest wartime landscapes are in fact views of small fishing ports on the Atlantic coast of Britain. In addition to the series of Polperro oils (e.g. Nos. 73, 76) which were painted from the terrace of his cottage, he made coloured pencil sketches of Nevin in North Wales, Port William in south-west Scotland, and the less enclosed harbour of Ullapool on the north-west Scottish coast, where he also painted the oil *Ullapool* (private collection). Heppenstall's landscape-body analogy is not inappropriate to Kokoschka's work. While his cityscapes have been likened to living human profiles marked by time, so his landscapes occasionally seem to suggest an anthropomorphic element. Kokoschka himself wrote in his autobiography that 'All landscapes are given their shape by man; without a human vision no one can know what the world really is.[42]

By the summer of 1940 foreigners, friendly or otherwise, were no longer allowed to remain in coastal areas, especially if they were close to important naval bases (Polperro is near Plymouth). Regulations had already come into force about photographing, sketching or painting sites designated as 'restricted', for which a written permit had to be obtained from the highest authority. In retrospect we may be grateful for these restrictions, since they forced Kokoschka to turn his mind to a medium, watercolour, which he had hardly touched since the 1920s. Back in London in September 1940, with the Blitz just beginning, he produced the first of many fresh and delicate still-lifes of cut flowers, thereby maintaining a symbolic link with nature until he was able once again to go out into the real landscape.

This became possible a year later, when he and Olda, by then married, were invited to stay with friends in Galloway. It was the first of half a dozen visits over the next five summers (and one spring) to this remote region of lowland Scotland, with its stony, rather flat moorland dotted with sheep and cattle. In 1944 and 1945 they also went further north to Ullapool, which in peacetime had been a thriving centre of the herring industry but which was now a restricted area where convoys were assembled and commandos trained. Here they discovered some of the most ancient and spectacular scenery in the British Isles.

In London, much of Kokoschka's time was taken up with political activity, making speeches, writing articles for anti-Nazi refugee newspapers, and helping to raise funds. His abhorrence of nationalism, coupled with his own unique personal history — born an Austrian, regarded by many as a major German artist, but holding Czech citizenship — made him the ideal figure to bestride the various refugee political organizations, who tended to keep to themselves when they did not openly squabble. But his role was far from being merely symbolic. He threw himself into the campaign for an independent and democratic Austria after the war, an objective recognized by the Allies at the Moscow conference in 1943, and he became involved in the activities of Young Austria, the youth section of the Free Austrian Movement. During Austro-Soviet Friendship week in June 1942, Young Austria collected a large proportion of the £3,600 needed to buy two mobile X-ray units for the Red Army. The following year Kokoschka donated the £1,000 he received for his portrait of Maisky, the Soviet Ambassador (No. 83), to the Stalingrad Hospital Fund, idealistically stipulating that it be used to treat both the Russian and German wounded. When his portrait of Masaryk was sold in New York in 1944, he set up a fund for the war orphans of Czechoslovakia with the proceeds, at a time when he could ill afford to be so generous. In 1946 he was still trying to raise money for humanitarian causes — in this case 'for the Viennese children who are starving'. In an open letter to the critic Alfred Neumayer published in the American *Magazine of Art,* he declared his intention to find £1,000 in the USA

> for a political painting I did in 1943, with the title: *What We are Fighting For.* It is a large and striking work. If you know somebody or some institution interested in it I would like to send you a photograph of it ...[43]

The ironically titled *'What We Are Fighting For'* (No. 82) was actually the last, and certainly the most complex, in a series of pictures satirising the war and the conduct of both axis and allied powers, which Kokoschka painted between 1939 and 1943 (Nos. 76, 78, 79, 80, 81, 82). The first, and least political, of these (No. 76) is also the most autobiographical. Towering over Polperro harbour a large and malevolent-looking spider crab threatens the tiny, vulnerable figure of the swimmer trying to reach the safety of the pier. Kokoschka said that the crab was a symbol for Chamberlain after Munich and that the swimmer represented Czechoslovakia.[44] The experience of meeting and painting Masaryk in Prague had deepened and enriched Kokoschka's art to a degree that became evident only now, when he felt an even stronger urge to clarify his intellectual and moral position. He proceeded to draw on various pictorial sources, including Brueghel, baroque allegory and a specifically English tradition, that of political caricature, with its crowded figure compositions, discrepancies of scale, crude imagery, animal and food symbolism, use of inscriptions and so on. It has been suggested that Kokoschka may have based the subject of *The Red Egg* (No. 78) — though not its more painterly treatment — on Gillray's satire *The Plumb-pudding in Danger,* 1805, which shows Pitt and Napoleon greedily carving up the globe.[45] That Kokoschka was familiar with early nineteenth-century English political cartoons is confirmed by the fact that he sent Michael Croft an inscribed copy of F. D. Klingender's *Russia — Britain's Ally: 1812–1942* for Christmas in 1942. The book carried an introduction by the Soviet Ambassador Maisky, who was sitting to Kokoschka at the time; in it he pointed to certain parallels between Napoleon in 1812 and Hitler in 1942. There followed an essay by Klingender and over fifty reproductions of popular caricatures by English and Russian artists past and present. Kokoschka knew Klingender, a Marxist art-historian who organized an exhibition of *Hogarth and English Caricature* under the auspices of the A.I.A. (Artists International Association) in the summer of 1943. Kokoschka admired Hogarth and in *Marianne-Maquis* (No. 81) reveals his knowledge of the scenes of lethargy and corruption in *A Rake's Progress* and *Marriage à la Mode.*[46]

The sarcastic political allegories represent a brief but intense phase in which Kokoschka perceived his art as having a didactic function. At one point in 1941 he was anxious to produce *The Red Egg* in poster form, as emerges from a letter to Michael Croft.

> Some friends of mine help together so that I can now print my Mussolini — Hitler caricature 'Appeasement' in colours and original size ... And I will be the first one to have started a Redcross help for it [the Red Army] in selling my print for the benefit of the fighters.[47]

How effective *The Red Egg* would have looked

translated into the flatter medium of lithography is open to doubt. Kokoschka's agitated brushwork, which vitalizes the image and conveys the strength of the artist's emotion, would certainly have suffered; and the clashing, high-key colours, so finely judged in the original, might have seemed cheap and vulgar. But Kokoschka clearly wanted to reach a wider public. His chance came in 1945, when he found the money to print his drawing of a baroque Christ, based on a statue on the Charles Bridge by Matthias Braun, leaning down from the cross to comfort a group of children. Along the crossbeam are inscribed the words 'IN MEMORY of the CHILDREN of EUROPE WHO HAVE to DIE OF COLD and HUNGER this XMAS'. Over a thousand (some say as many as 5,000) copies of this simple, moving image were put up in the London Underground and on the buses in December 1945. At an earlier stage Kokoschka seems to have been under the impression that it would be 'posted everywhere in England by the Church'.[48] For the artist, the significance of the poster lay in the fact that, as he wrote to a friend, 'there is no organization, nor Party, nor collect mentioned'.[49] However committed, his art never descended to the level of ideological propaganda.

The loose, nervous handling of the political paintings is also apparent in the few portraits Kokoschka painted at this time, among which those of the young Michael Croft, his sister Rosemary (Nos. 74, 75) and Countess Drogheda (No. 85) are outstanding. In the two Croft pictures Kokoschka paints skin almost as if it were raw flesh, anticipating his own searing self-portrait of 1948 (No. 87) and the even more livid complexions of some later subjects. Rayner Heppenstall was the first to observe the deliberately allusive character of these new works.

> ... the background contains figures, landscape and symbolical images. Kokoschka will never do a portrait of anybody whom he dislikes or to whom he is indifferent. In the case of strangers to whom he may have taken a fancy, he will ask for photographs of their parents and themselves and will not begin work until he feels that he understands their history. Childhood scenes and faces of parents are likely to appear in the finished portraits.[50]

Although the Kokoschkas did not finally settle at Villeneuve, on the eastern shore of Lac Léman in Switzerland, until September 1953, from the spring of 1947, when Oskar's first post-war retrospective opened at Basel, they were almost continually on the move throughout continental Europe. In 1949 Kokoschka flew to the USA for the first time, to see the big travelling exhibition of his work there and also to teach at the Tanglewood Summer School near Boston, which in retrospect can be seen as the prototype of his School of Seeing at Salzburg.

As the war neared its end, Kokoschka's mood, instead of growing more optimistic, had darkened. He and Olda

Kokoschka with Olda, Venice, 1948 (photo: Ferruzzi).

were concerned about the fate of their relatives in Vienna and Prague, of whom there was no news. When word finally arrived, it was not promising: 'Prague is very bare of all food and clothing'; 'Vienna ... seems to be worse off than any other part of the continent, no food at all and no contact possible'.[51] Their energies were devoted to writing, making enquiries and sending parcels of food, medicine and clothing by circuitous routes. On an international level, the allied bombing of Dresden, in part to placate Stalin, appalled Kokoschka, as did the dropping of the first atomic bomb on the Japanese, an event he spurned as 'the logical conclusion of a mathematical attitude towards social problems'.[52] The future of eastern Europe seemed to him unutterably bleak: '... they drive wholesale men, women, old and young, babies and sick ones out from the countries with no land where to go. Millions of people die on the road'.[53] He was particularly worried about his sister in Prague, whom he succeeded in visiting in 1946 on the death of her husband. Over three million German-speaking Czechs had recently been expel-

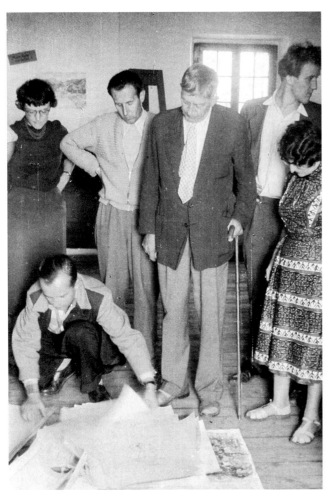

Kokoschka teaching at the School of Seeing, Salzburg, 1954 (photo: E. H. Gombrich).

Painting the portrait of Theodor Körner, Mayor of Vienna, 1949.

led from the country, which within two years was under firm communist control.

Kokoschka's letter to Alfred Neumayer, published in 1946, is typical of several in which he expressed feelings of disillusionment and despair.

> ... the kind of world I would like to return to, my world in which I travelled as a happy tramp, does not exist any longer. Big towns have disappeared from the surface of the earth, great countries left as deserts. There is no end yet even of the murdering, which now goes on in a cold systematic way, no less inhuman than the murdering with weapons and machinery. Power politics extended the hunger-blockade after the 'cease fire'. To the destruction of cultural documents (of my home town, Vienna, only shabby remains tell of its former glory) the annihilation of humanistic values is connected in a way that makes seem normal today the callous views towards human life which we despised in Fascism ... What Hitler sowed is ripening. His insane mind conceived the idea of the collective guilt, and, unfortunately, the post-war world sticks to this delusion of a madman, dispensing justice on such conceptions. I cannot live in such a world![54]

The 1947 exhibition at Basel, however, marked a turning-point. Its huge success gave Kokoschka back his 'joie de vivre, faith in humanity, and hope for the future', as he told his sister.[55] Kokoschka was now sixty-one and had just become a British subject. Over the remaining twenty-five years or so of his creative life he emerged as a public figure — to some a prophet — who spoke out against the dehumanizing effect of mass society wherever he detected it, in art as much as politics. Social engineering, belief in technological progress and, not least, standardized patterns of thought were evils which would lead to the 'suicide of society'. At Salzburg where he taught every summer from 1953 to 1963 he was at last able to put his antirationalist philosophy of learning through seeing — his language of the eye — to the test. Confronted by the rising tide of what he pointedly referred to as 'non-objective' art, he alone reiterated the importance of content and of the dynamic representation of space and light in painting. Respect for tradition, for the inheritance of Greece and Rome, became an integral part of his credo. In his great monumental works of the early 1950s on the subject of freedom, *The Promethus Saga* and *Thermopylae* triptychs, he understood his mission as one of defending 'the artistic tradition of Europe'.[56]

Kokoschka continued to paint portraits. Beginning in 1949 with Theodor Körner, Mayor of Vienna and later President of Austria, his subjects included many of the architects of post-war European reconstruction as well as a series of people in old age, not least himself. His townscapes became ever more atmospheric and broken in style, the best of them, such as *Berlin, 13 August 1966* and *New York* (No. 99), evoking a cosmic or apoca-

Kokoschka with Konrad Adenauer, 1966.

Painting Berlin from the top of the Axel Springer tower, August 1966.

In front of his *Thermopylae* triptych, Tate Gallery, 1962
(photo: Horst Tappe).

In the garden at Villeneuve, Easter 1960
(Kokoschka archive, Villeneuve).

lyptic dimension. As its relationship to ecstatic baroque rhythms grew more explicit, the visionary power of Kokoschka's painting intensified. In December 1953, shortly before starting work on the *Thermopylae* triptych, he advised his pupil Philip Moysey to copy Rubens's *The Judgment of Paris* in the National Gallery, London.

You ought to learn about the different ways of his wonderful brush, how he paints light, skin, complexion, the grey half-tones beneath the overlaying lustre and last touches. Sometimes he started with a tempera-white design, always used a reddish flesh-tone background, different layers, which you only can see, adore and get drunken with ... when you are trying to copy it.[57]

In their robustness and vitality, the pictures on classical and mythological themes, such as *Herodotus* (No. 97) or the massive *Theseus and Antiope* (No. 107), rank with the grandest and most ambitious of Kokoschka's earlier works. The bright, powdery colours (especially scarlet and yellow), the spontaneous application of paint, and, after he had passed his eightieth birthday, the poignant allegories of the artist as an old man approaching death — all the hallmarks of a distinctive late style are present, comparable to Picasso's in its freedom and reckless disregard of academic norms.

Interviewing Kokoschka at the time of his Tate Gallery retrospective in 1962, Andrew Forge put it to the artist that 'the total sum of your work is like a painting of the whole world, as though you had tried to embrace the whole world, its cities, its people, its condition'.[58] The key to Kokoschka's *Weltanschauung* is best provided by those who sat to him or were taught by him. Gitta Wallerstein recalled that 'While he was working he was a lover towards his subject — both men and women ...'[59] His English pupils Philip Moysey and Ishbel McWhirter both remember him as an intuitive teacher who recommended them to ignore irrelevant prosaic detail and concentrate on the essentials of a person or scene. 'You have eyes, use them, love what you see', he told Moysey.[60] The word 'love' also occurs in Kokoschka's letters to McWhirter.

My advice is to portray as sincerely and well [as] you can do it — again and again! It will ease the tension and make you more human as an artist because love is the best teacher.[61]

It may sound trite or sentimental to talk about an artist's compassion, but there is no doubt that emotion, and not intellectual theory, was the basis of Kokoschka's teaching as it was of his art. His interest in children was informed by precisely similar feelings. As a student at the School of Applied Arts in Vienna he had fallen under the spell of Franz Cizek, the pioneer of children's art education, who encouraged his classes to draw freely from their imagination as opposed to making sterile academic copies. Cizek was one of the first to take child art seriously; a room of his pupils' work was included in the 1908 *Kunstschau*, at which Kokoschka exhibited his illustrated 'fairy-tale' *The Dreaming Youths*. When Kokoschka was employed as a drawing master at Eugenie Schwarzwald's progressive school in 1911–12, he adopted some of Cizek's methods. His understanding of Comenius, as we have seen, convinced him of the necessity of allowing a child to develop naturally through direct experience of the world, helped by pictures, demonstrations, games and other visual and practical aids. In London during the war Kokoschka opened two exhibitions of children's art, at which he outlined the educational ideas of both Cizek and Comenius. The second of these, *The War as seen by Children,* was organized by the Refugee Children's Evacuation Fund, of which the educationalist A. S. Neill was a patron. Drawings by Neill's pupils at Summerhill were exhibited at the Arcade Gallery in London in 1944; and in April 1945 Kokoschka spent three weeks at another famous progressive school, Dartington Hall in Devon.

The School of Seeing, in other words, was the culmination of a lifelong concern with the nature and value of education. In 1941 Kokoschka wrote that 'The main task of democracy is to realize the universal debt of the old men to the youth of the world'.[62] At the School of Seeing he discharged that debt and inspired a whole generation.

NOTES

1. 'Oskar Kokoschka Looks Back: A conversation with Andrew Forge', *The Listener*, 20 September 1962, p. 425.

2. From the beginning, critics have compared the 'disgusting' sulphurous colours in Kokoschka's depiction of skin to those of Grünewald in the Isenheim Altarpiece. See, recently, Alfred Werner, 'Kokoschka at Ninety'. *American Artist*, April 1976, p. 35.

3. By Herbert Furst in *Portrait Painting, its Nature and Function*, London 1927, p. 139.

4. Conversation with Andrew Forge, p. 425 (see note 1 above).

5. Paul Stefan (intro.), *Oskar Kokoschka, Dramen und Bilder*, Leipzig 1913; quoted after Frank Whitford, *Oskar Kokoschka, a Life*, London 1986, p. 78. Stefan was one of the first to compare Kokoschka's portraits to caricature: '... he could not see people, only animals and spirits. And for him the human face became a caricature...'.

6. Edith Hoffmann, *Kokoschka, Life and Work*, London 1947, p. 103.

7. Henrik Ibsen, *Ghosts and Other Plays*, Harmondsworth 1964, p. 228 (translated by Peter Watts). This comparison was suggested to me by Professor Ernst Gombrich.

8. Ulrich Conrads (ed.) *Programmes and manifestoes on 20th century architecture*, London 1970, p. 32.

9. Hoffmann, *op cit.*, p. 115.

10. In a letter dated 24 November 1949 to an American student, published in *Oskar Kokoschka Briefe III 1934–1953*, edited by Olda Kokoschka and Heinz Spielmann, Düsseldorf 1986, pp. 236–9. In all fairness, Kokoschka distances himself in this letter from the modern cult of El Greco.

11. Kokoschka refers to the project in the interview with Andrew Forge (see note 1 above): 'And so I thought the colour must be large enough to reach people 200 yards away, or more; it must carry. So I had to study colour; the effect of light, and the harmonies of colours.' (p. 427). See also J. P. Hodin, *Oskar Kokoschka, the Artist and his Time*, London 1966, pp. 109, 165.

12. Oskar Kokoschka, *My Life*, London 1974, p. 123.

13. Hoffmann, p. 189.

14. Conversation with Forge, p. 427.

15. Hoffmann, p. 178.

16. *My Life*, p. 129.

17. *Oskar Kokoschka, Briefe II, 1919–1934*, edited by Olda Kokoschka and Heinz Spielmann, Düsseldorf 1985, p. 137.

18. *Ibid.*, p. 138; letter to Marguerite Loeb.

19. *Ibid.*, p. 151; letter to Romana Kokoschka.

20. *Ibid.*, pp. 152–53.

21. *Ibid.*, p. 158; letter to Anna Kallin.

22. T. W. Earp 'Fog and Fireworks', *The New Statesman*, 23 June 1928, p. 358. Walter Bayes was even more derogatory, singling out Konody's introduction for particular scorn ('Imports and Exports in the Arts', *The Saturday Review*, 23 June 1928, pp. 802–3).

23. See, for example, Hoffmann, p. 178; Peter Selz, *German Expressionist Painting*, Berkeley and Los Angeles, 1974 edition, p. 253; Hodin, *op cit.*, p. 171.

24. Hoffmann, p. 25.

25. Conversation with Forge, p. 426.

26. Quoted after Whitford, *op cit.*, p. 149.

27. In a post-card to Ishbel McWhirter postmarked 10 September 1948 Kokoschka referred to the École de Paris, 'where even the fashion dressers give up and settle for mass-production in New York. Paris is bankrupt just as French painting'.

28. John also supported the Young Austria movement in Britain: see correspondence in the Archives of the Austrian Resistance, Vienna.

29. 'How I See Myself', *Oskar Kokoschka: early drawings and watercolours*, London 1985, p. 24; originally published in German as 'Der Bürgerschreck Kokoschka', *Die neue Weltbühne*, Prague, 12 March 1936, pp. 335–39.

30. See note 24 above. Kokoschka suggested as a provisional title for the Wilhelminenberg painting 'The Five Senses' (letter to Wolfgang Gurlitt, 18 September 1932).

31. Hoffmann, p. 197.

32. Letter to F K Gotsch, 1 November 1934, published in *Oskar Kokoschka Briefe III 1934–1953*, edited by Olda Kokoschka and Heinz Spielmann, Düsseldorf 1986, p. 9.

33. Letter in English to Homer Saint Gaudens, 21 September 1940: *ibid.*, p. 100.

34. *Prager Tagblatt*, 8 September 1935.

35. Letter to Edith Hoffmann, 24 November 1937 (Kokoschka Archive, Villeneuve).

36. *Zeitspiegel, anti-Nazi weekly*, 22 December 1941, p. 3.

37. Letter to Anna Kallin, early February 1936, *Briefe III*, pp. 28–29.

38. Letter to Philip Moysey, June (?) 1940 (copy in Tate Gallery Archive).

39. F.G., 'Oskar Kokoschka', *The Spectator*, 20 March 1936, p. 513.

40. Letter to Hilde Goldschmidt, 30 August 1939 (Kokoschka Archive, Villeneuve).

41. Rayner Heppenstall, *Saturnine*, London 1943, p. 124.

42. *My Life*, p. 167.

43. 'A Letter from Oskar Kokoschka', *Magazine of Art*, May 1946, p. 196.

44. See Edward Beddington-Behrens, *Look Back, Look Forward*, London 1963, p. 168.

45. Robert Radford, 'Kokoschka's Political Painting in Britain', typescript of an unpublished lecture, 1983, p. 4.

46. Kokoschka mentioned his admiration for Hogarth to Michael Croft in November-December 1938, while painting his portrait. Works by Hogarth, Gillray and Brueghel are illustrated in *Caricature* by E. H. Gombrich and Ernst Kris (King Penguin, Harmondsworth 1940), a book which Kokoschka might also have known, given that both its authors were Viennese emigrés (Gombrich later became a friend).

47. Letter to the Hon. Michael Croft, late 1941.

48. Note to Emil Korner written on the back of a related sketch for Kokoschka's Christmas card, 1945.

49. *Ibid.*

50. Heppenstal, *op cit.*, pp. 127–28.

51. Letters from Olda Kokoschka to Constance Mitford, 6 June and 2 August 1945 (copies in Tate Gallery Archive).

52. Letter to Philip Moysey, 30 August 1945, *Briefe III*, p. 148.

53. *Ibid.*

54. See note 43 above.

55. Letter to Berta Patocková, 31 March 1947, *Briefe III*, p. 183.

56. Translations of Kokoschka's explanatory texts on the two triptychs are published in Hodin, *op cit.*, pp. 190–93.

57. Letter to Philip Moysey, 20 December 1953 (copy in Tate Gallery Archive).

58. *Loc. cit.*, p. 426.

59. Gitta Wallerstein's reminiscenses are to be found in Hodin, pp. 155–59.

60. Philip Moysey, in *Kokoschka: People and Places*, 8 pp. broadsheet, Tate Gallery, London 1986.

61. Postcard to Ishbel McWhirter, 20 May 1949 (copy in Tate Gallery Archive).

62. 'Children's Art Exhibition', *Oskar Kokoschka, Politische Äußerungen. Das schriftliche Werk*, vol. IV, edited by Heinz Spielmann, Hamburg 1976, p. 211. In the same speech, Kokoschka refers to Cizek as 'an old teacher of mine' (p. 209).

Kokoschka in 1974 (photo: Derry Moore).

BIOGRAPHY

1886 Born 1 March at Pöchlarn, c.100 km west of Vienna on the Danube. Second of four children of Prague-born goldsmith Gustav Kokoschka and of Romana Loidl, a forester's daughter from Hollenstein in the Lower Austrian Alps. Childhood and youth spent in Vienna.

1904 Takes Matura examination at Währinger Staatsrealschule, in Vienna's 18th district. Awarded state scholarship to study at the *Kunstgewerbeschule* of the Austrian Museum for Art and Industry.

1907 Becomes associate of the *Wiener Werkstätte*. Starts work on his illustrated poem *Die träumenden Knaben*. Makes shadow puppets for WW's Cabaret Fledermaus in Vienna.

1908 Gives regular evening class in drawing at the *Kunstgewerbeschule*. Invited to exhibit at the *Kunstschau* by the Klimt circle.

Publication of *Die träumenden Knaben*, dedicated to Klimt. Meets architect Adolf Loos and gradually moves away from WW.

1909 Participates in the *Internationale Kunstschau* where his play *Mörder Hoffnung der Frauen* is performed. Leaves *Kunstgewerbeschule*. Begins a series of 'psychological' portraits of, among others, Loos, Karl Kraus and Peter Altenberg.

Accompanies Loos to Switzerland.

1910 Paints portraits of T. B. patients in a Swiss sanatorium. Spends most of the year in Berlin, contributing texts and drawings to Herwarth Walden's *Der Sturm*. First important exhibition at Paul Cassirer's gallery; first one-man show at the Folkwang Museum, Hagen.

1911 Returns to Vienna. Included in the *Hagenbund's* exhibition of contemporary art from Austria, Germany and Switzerland.

Teaches drawing part-time at Eugenie Schwarzwald's progressive girls' school in Vienna. Contact with the *Blaue Reiter*.

1912 Exhibits at Walden's *Sturm* gallery in Berlin. Shows six works in the international *Sonderbund* exhibition in Cologne. Start of passionate relationship with Alma Mahler, the composer's widow, with whom he travels to Switzerland in the summer. Teaches life drawing at the *Kunstgewerbeschule* in Vienna.

1913 Travels to Italy with Alma Mahler. In Vienna, starts work on the painting *Die Windsbraut (The Tempest)*. Leaves *Kunstgewerbeschule*.

1914 Enlists in the Dragoons.

1915 Military training. End of affair with Alma Mahler. Sent to the Eastern front, where he is badly wounded. Hospitalised in Vienna.

1916 Serves as a liaison officer on the Slovenian-Italian front. War drawings. Travels to Germany and signs contract with Cassirer. Publication of portfolios *Bach-Kantate* and *Der gefesselte Kolumbus*. Convalescence at sanatorium in Weisser Hirsch district of Dresden. Friendship with Expressionist writers and actors.

1917 Zurich Dada artists perform Kokoschka's play *Hiob*. Visits Sweden.

1918 Commissions life-size doll in the likeness of Alma Mahler. First one-man show at Cassirer's gallery in Berlin.

1919 Appointed Professor of painting at the Dresden Academy. Begins a series of views of the River Elbe (*Dresden, Neustadt I* etc).

1920 Buys family a house on the outskirts of Vienna.

1921 Meets Anna Kallin, his companion until 1925.

1922 Represents Germany at the Venice Biennale with Liebermann, Slevogt and Corinth.

1923 Leaves Dresden; travels to Switzerland with Anna Kallin. Death of Kokoschka's father.

1924–30 Travels in Italy, France, Spain, Switzerland, Holland, Britain, Ireland, North Africa and the Middle East, resulting in numerous landscapes and townscapes, including the first of many paintings of the River Thames.

1931 Extensive stay in Paris; one-man show at the Galerie Georges Petit. Dissolution of contract with Cassirer's. Returns to Vienna where the city authorities commission a painting (*View from the Wilhelminenberg*). Begins series of 'Trudl' pictures.

1933 Hitler becomes Chancellor of Germany. Kokoschka publishes article defending Liebermann against Nazi persecution.

1934 Civil war in Vienna followed by the end of democratic government in Austria. Death of Kokoschka's mother. Moves to Prague where he paints the first of several views of the city. Meets Olda Palkovská.

1935 Political and humanist writings. Starts work on portrait of the Czech President Thomas G. Masaryk, who helps Kokoschka apply for Czech citizenship.

1937 Retrospective exhibition in Vienna. Eight paintings included in the Nazi exhibition *Entartete 'Kunst'* in Munich. By the end of the year over 400 works of Kokoschka's confiscated from German museums. Begins *Self-portrait of a 'Degenerate Artist'*.

1938 Hitler's annexation of Austria (13 March). Munich Agreement (29 September). Kokoschka and Olda Palkovská emigrate to London.

1939 Moves to Polperro (Cornwall). Begins series of anti-war pictures.

1940 Returns to London. Throughout the war, actively involved in anti-Nazi emigré organisations.

1941 Marries Olda Palkovská. First of several wartime excursions to Scotland, where he produces watercolours and his first drawings in coloured pencil.

1942 Begins portrait of Ivan Maisky, Soviet Ambassador to Britain. Donates fee for this and subsequent paintings to humanitarian causes.

1943 Paints *What We Are Fighting For*, the last, and most ironical, of his anti-war allegories.

1947 Adopts British nationality. First large post-war retrospective in Basel and Zurich.

1948 Special exhibition at the Venice Biennale. First important exhibition in the U.S.A.

1949 Paints portrait of Theodor Körner, Mayor of Vienna. First visit to the U.S.A.

1950 Retrospective in Munich. Paints *The Prometheus Saga* triptych for Count Seilern in London.

1953 Foundation of International Summer School for the Visual Arts at Salzburg. Kokoschka takes a painting course, which he calls the *Schule des Sehens*, every year until 1963.

Leaves London and settles in the house he and Olda have had built at Villeneuve above Lake Geneva in Switzerland.

1954 Commissioned to design sets and costumes for Wilhelm Furtwängler's production of *The Magic Flute*. Paints *Thermopylae* triptych for Hamburg University.

1956 First visit to Greece.

1958 Major retrospectives in Munich, Vienna and The Hague.

1960 Awarded the Erasmus Prize.

1961 Travels to Greece.

1962 Important retrospective at the Tate Gallery, London.

1963 Travels to Apulia in southern Italy.

Publication of *King Lear* portfolio (lithographs).

1964 Lithographic cycle *Bekenntnis zu Hellas* published.

1965 Publication of *Die Odyssee* lithographs.

1966 Paints portrait of Konrad Adenauer.

Commissioned by Axel Springer to paint view of Berlin on fifth anniversary of the building of the Wall. Travels to New York and paints view of Manhattan. Large retrospective to mark Kokoschka's eightieth birthday held in Zurich.

1968 Visits Turkey.

1969 Publication of *Saul and David* and *Die Frösche* print cycles.

1970 Etchings for Kleist's *Penthesilea* published.

1971 Major retrospective at the Upper Belvedere in Vienna. Kokoschka's autobiography *Mein Leben* published.

1972 Works on cartoons for mosaic *Ecce Homo (Ecce Homines)* for St. Nikolai church in Hamburg. Travels to Greece.

1973 Travels to Jerusalem and makes portrait drawings for the Jerusalem Foundation.

Opening of the *Oskar Kokoschka-Dokumentation* at Pöchlarn, the artist's birthplace.

1975 Drawings for final lithographic cycles *Comenius* and *Pan*.

1976 Exhibitions to celebrate his 90th birthday.

1978 Major touring exhibition in Japan.

1980 Dies 22 February at Montreux in Switzerland.

BIBLIOGRAPHY

1. Books and portfolios (including works illustrated by the artist).

Jagdbuch (Diarium). Vienna: Wiener Werkstätte, 1908.

Die träumenden Knaben. (The dreaming youths.) Vienna: Wiener Werkstätte, 1908.

Zwanzig Zeichnungen. Berlin: Der Sturm, 1913.

Dramen und Bilder. Leipzig: Kurt Wolff, 1913; introd. by Paul Stefan. Contains the plays *Mörder Hoffnung der Frauen* (Murderer Hope of Women), *Sphinx und Strohmann* (Sphinx and Strawman) and *Schauspiel* (A play).

Mörder Hoffnung der Frauen. Berlin: Der Sturm, 1916.

Der gefesselte Kolumbus. (Columbus in chains.) Berlin: Fritz Gurlitt, 1916. Portfolio of 12 lithographs illustrating Kokoschka's dramatic poem.

Menschenköpfe. (People's heads.) Berlin: Der Sturm, 1916. Portfolio of 15 etchings.

O Ewigkeit — Du Donnerwort; Wörte der Kantate nach Johann Sebastian Bach. (Eternity, thou fearful word: text of Bach's Cantata.) Berlin: Fritz Gurlitt, 1916 & 1917. Portfolio of 9 lithographs and poem *Zueignung* (Dedication); publ. in book-form by Fritz Gurlitt, 1918, in series 'Die Neuen Bilderbücher, 1. Reihe'.

Der brennende Dornbusch; Mörder Hoffnung der Frauen. (The Burning Bush; Murderer Hope of Women). Leipzig: Kurt Wolff, 1917.

Hiob. (Job.) Berlin: Paul Cassirer, 1917. Play, with 14 lithographs.

Vier Dramen. (Four plays.) Berlin: Paul Cassirer, 1919. Contains the plays *Orpheus und Eurydike, Der brennende Dornbusch, Mörder Hoffnung der Frauen* and *Hiob*.

Der gefesselte Kolumbus. Berlin: Fritz Gurlitt (series 'Die Neuen Bilderbücher, 3. Reihe'), 1921; book edition of 1916 portfolio.

Variationen über ein Thema. Vienna: R. Lanyi; Vienna, Prague, Leipzig: Strache, 1921; introd. by Max Dvorak; ed. by Bohuslav Kokoschka. Portfolio containing 4 p. text and 10 photogravure reproductions of drawings by Kokoschka.

Orpheus und Eurydice. Vienna, New York: Universal Edition, 1925. Play in 3 acts by Kokoschka, music by Ernst Křenek.

Handzeichnungen. Berlin: Rathenau, 1935; ed. by Ernest Rathenau.

Ann Eliza Reed. Hamburg: Maximilian-Presse, 1952. Story with 10 lithographs.

Schriften 1907–1955. Munich: Albert Langen-Müller, 1956; ed. by H.M. Wingler.

Thermopylae: ein Triptychon. Winterthur: BW-Presse, 1955. Text by Kokoschka & Walter Kern.

Spur in Treibsand: Geschichten. Zürich: Atlantis, 1956.

Handzeichnungen. Berlin: Rathenau, 1961; introd. by P. Westheim; ed. by Ernest Rathenau. Publ. as *Drawings*, London: Thames and Hudson, 1962.

A sea ringed with visions. London: Thames and Hudson, 1962. Stories told to Olda.

Bekenntnis zu Hellas. (Homage to Hellas). London: Marlborough Fine Art, 1964. 2 portfolios of 26 lithographs.

Apulia. London: Marlborough Fine Art, 1964. Series of 20 lithographs.

Die Odyssee. London: Ganymed Original Editions & Marlborough Fine Art, 1965. Series of 44 lithographs.

Marrakesch. London: Marlborough Fine Art, 1966. Portfolio of 18 lithographs.

Handzeichnungen/Drawings 1906–1965. New York: Ernest Rathenau, 1966; republ. Coral Gables (Fla): University of Miami Press, 1970; ed. by Ernest Rathenau; introduction by Kokoschka.

Saul und David. London: Ganymed Original Editions & Marlborough Fine Art, 1969. Series of 41 lithographs.

'Die Frösche' des Aristophanes. (Aristophanes's 'The Frogs'). Frankfurt a.M.: G. de Beauclair, 1969. Series of 12 etchings, as portfolio & in book-form.

Penthesilea. Frankfurt a.M.: G. de Beauclair, 1970. Drama by Heinrich von Kleist with 10 etchings by Kokoschka.

Saul and David. London: Thames and Hudson, 1973. Text of 2 Books of Samuel with lithographs by Kokoschka; book edition of 1969 portfolio.

Mein Leben. Munich: Bruckmann, 1971; tr. as *My Life*, London: Thames and Hudson, 1974.

Handzeichnungen 1906–1969. New York: Ernest Rathenau, 1971; introd. by Carl Georg Heise in collaboration with the artist.

The women of Troy. London: Marlborough Graphics, 1973. Series of 13 lithographs illustrating Euripides' tragedy.

Das schriftliche Werk, vols. I–IV. Hamburg: Christians, 1973–76; ed. by Heinz Spielmann.

Pan. Hamburg: Hoffmann und Campe, 1978. Portfolio of 17 lithographs illustrating Knut Hamsun's novel.

Briefe, vols. I–IV. Düsseldorf: Claasen, 1984–87; ed. by Olda Kokoschka & Heinz Spielmann.

2. Books on the artist.

Paul Westheim. *Oskar Kokoschka*. Potsdam-Berlin: Gustav Kiepenhauer, 1918.

Paul Westheim. *Oskar Kokoschka*. Berlin: Paul Cassirer, 1925.

Georg Biermann. *Oskar Kokoschka*. Leipzig, Berlin: Klinkhardt und Biermann ('Junge Kunst', Band 52), 1929.

Hans Heilmaier. *Oskar Kokoschka*. Paris: G. Grès & Cie. ('Les artistes nouveaux'), 1929.

Hans Platschek. *Oskar Kokoschka*. Buenos Aires: Poseidon ('Biblioteca Argentina de Arte'), 1946.

Edith Hoffmann. *Kokoschka: life and work*. London: Faber & Faber, 1947; incl. 2 essays by Kokoschka & a foreword by Herbert Read.

James S. Plaut. *Oskar Kokoschka*. Boston: Institute of Contemporary Art; London: Max Parrish, 1948.

Paul Westheim. *Oskar Kokoschka: Landschaften*. Zürich: Rascher, 1948.

Doris Wild. *Oskar Kokoschka: Blumenaquarelle*. Zürich: Rascher, 1948.

Michelangelo Masciotta. *Kokoschka*. Florence: Del Turco, 1949.

Doris Thurston. *Notes on Kokoschka*. New York: Chappaqua, 1950.

Hans M. Wingler. *Oskar Kokoschka: Orbis pictus, I et II*. Salzburg: Galerie Welz, 1951.

Paul Westheim. *Oskar Kokoschka: Gestalten und Landschaften*. Zürich: Rascher, 1952.

Hans M. Wingler. *Künstler und Poeten: Zeichnungen von Oskar Kokoschka*. Feldafing: Buchheim, 1954.

Bernhard Paumgartner. *Oskar Kokoschka: Zeichnungen für die Bühnenausstattung für W.A. Mozarts 'Zauberflöte'* (Salzburger Festspiele 1955–56). Salzburg: Galerie Welz, 1955.

Hans M. Wingler. *Oskar Kokoschka: ein Lebensbild in zeitgenössischen Dokumenten*. Munich: Albert Langen, Georg Müller, 1956.

Hans M. Wingler. *Oskar Kokoschka: das Werk des Malers*. Salzburg: Galerie Welz, 1956; tr. as *Oskar Kokoschka: the work of the painter*, London: Faber & Faber, 1958.

Hans M. Wingler. *Kokoschka-Fibel*. Salzburg: Galerie Welz, 1957; tr. as *Introduction to Kokoschka*, London: Thames and Hudson, 1958.

Bernhard Bultmann. *Oskar Kokoschka*. Salzburg: Galerie Welz, 1959; tr., London: Thames and Hudson, 1961.

Bernhard Borchert. *Kokoschka*. Berlin, 1959; tr., London: Faber & Faber, 1960.

Oskar Kokoschka: Thermopylae. Stuttgart: Reclam, 1961; introd. by Carl G. Heise; texts by Bruno Snell and the artist.

Oskar Kokoschka: watercolours, drawings, writings. London: Thames and Hudson, 1962; introd. by John Russell.

Ludwig Goldscheider. *Kokoschka*. London: Phaidon, 1963. Written in collaboration with the artist.

Joseph P. Hodin. *Bekenntnis zu Kokoschka: Erinnerungen und Deutungen*. Berlin, Mainz: Kupferberg, 1963.

Edgar Horstmann. *Oskar Kokoschka in Hamburg*. Hamburg: Christians, 1965.

Joseph P. Hodin. *Oskar Kokoschka: the artist and his time*. London: Cory, Adams & Mackay, 1966; tr. as *Oskar Kokoschka: sein Leben, seine Zeit*, Mainz: Kupferberg, 1968.

Fritz Schmalenbach. *Oskar Kokoschka*. Königstein im Taunus: Karl R. Langewiesche, Nachfolger Hans Koster, 1967.

Jan Tomeš. *Kokoschka: the artist in Prague*. London: Hamlyn, 1967.

Heinz Spielmann. *Oskar Kokoschka: die Fächer für Alma Mahler*. (The fans for Alma Mahler.) Hamburg, 1969.

Giuseppe Gatt. *Kokoschka*. Florence: Sansoni, 1970; tr., London, New York, Sydney, Toronto, 1971.

Gerhard J. Lischka. *Oskar Kokoschka: Maler und Dichter*. Bern, Frankfurt a.M.: Peter Lang, 1972.

Jan Tomeš. *Oskar Kokoschka: Londoner Ansichten, Englische Landschaften*. Munich: Bruckmann; tr. as *Oskar Kokoschka: London views, British landscapes*, London: Thames and Hudson, 1972.

Begegnung mit Kokoschka: eine Festschrift zur Eröffnung der Oskar Kokoschka Dokumentation Pöchlarn. Pöchlarn: Oskar Kokoschka Dokumentation, 1973.

Hans M. Wingler, Friedrich Welz. *Oskar Kokoschka: das druckgraphische Werk*. Salzburg: Galerie Welz, 1975.

Ivan Fenjö. *Oskar Kokoschka: die frühe Graphik*. Vienna: Euro-Art Bücherkreis, 1976.

Oskar Kokoschka: vom Erleben im Leben, Schriften und Bilder. Salzburg: Galerie Welz, 1976; ed. by Otto Breicha.

Friedrich Welz. *Oskar Kokoschka: frühe Druckgraphik, 1906–1912*. Salzburg: Galerie Welz, 1977.

Alfred Reisinger. *Kokoschka Dichtungen nach dem Expressionismus*. Vienna, Munich, Zürich: Europa-Verlag ('Beitrage zur österreichischen Kultur-und Geistesgeschichte', Band 2), 1978.

Hans M. Wingler, Friedrich Welz. *Oskar Kokoschka: das druckgraphische Werk II: Druckgraphik 1975–1980*. Salzburg: Galerie Welz, 1981. Supplement to 1975 catalogue raisonné.

Henry I. Schvey. *Oskar Kokoschka: the painter as playwright*. Detroit: Wayne State University Press, 1982.

Werner J. Schweiger. *Der junge Kokoschka: Leben und Werk 1904–1914*. Vienna, Munich: Christian Brandstätter, 1983.

Oskar Kokoschka: early drawings and watercolours. London: Thames and Hudson, 1985; introd. by Serge Sabarsky.

Heinz Spielmann. *Kokoschkas Fächer für Alma Mahler*. Dortmund: Die bibliophilen Taschenbücher, 1985.

Frank Whitford. *Oskar Kokoschka: a life*. London: Weidenfeld and Nicolson, 1986.

Richard Calvocoressi and others. *Oskar Kokoschka 1886–1980*, centenary exhibition catalogue. London: Tate Gallery, 1986.

E.H. Gombrich. *Kokoschka in his Time*. London: Tate Gallery, 1986.

E.H. Gombrich and Heinz Spielmann. *Oskar Kokoschka, the late work 1953–1980*, exhibition catalogue. London: Marlborough Fine Art, 1990.

ILLUSTRATIONS

1. *Still-life with Pineapple.* 1909.
   Oil on canvas, 42⅞ × 30¾ in. (109 × 78 cm).
   Staatliche Museen Preussischer Kulturbesitz, Nationalgalerie, Berlin.

1

2. *Father Hirsch.* 1909.
Oil on canvas, 27 ³/₄ × 24 ⁵/₈ in. (70.5 × 62.5 cm).
Neue Galerie der Stadt Linz, Wolfgang-Gurlitt-Museum.

3. *Martha Hirsch.* 1909.
   Oil on canvas, 34⅝ × 27⅝ in. (88 × 70 cm).
   Private Collection, U.S.A.

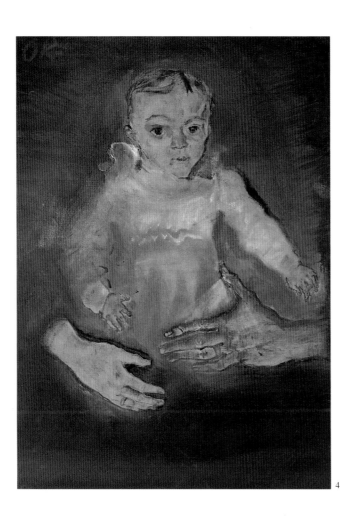

4

4. *Child with the Hands of its Father and Mother.* 1909.
   Oil on canvas, 28⅜ × 20½ in. (72 × 52 cm).
   Österreichische Galerie, Vienna.

5. *Children Playing.* 1909.
   Oil on canvas, 28⅜ × 42½ in. (72 × 108 cm).
   Wilhelm Lehmbruck Museum, Duisburg.

6. *Lotte Franzos.* 1909.
   Oil on canvas, 45¼ × 31¼ in. (115 × 79.5 cm).
   Phillips Collection, Washington, D.C.

5

7. *Felix Albrecht Harta.* 1909.
   Oil on canvas, 28¾ × 20⅝ in. (73.1 × 52.5 cm).
   Hirshhorn Museum and Sculpture Garden, Smithsonian Institution, Washington, D.C.

8. *Adolf Loos.* 1909.
    Oil on canvas, 29 1/8 × 35 7/8 in. (74×91 cm).
    Staatliche Museen Preussischer Kulturbesitz, Nationalgalerie, Berlin.

9. *Ludwig Ritter von Janikowski.* 1909.
   Oil on canvas, 23¾×22½ in. (60.2×57.2 cm).
   Private Collection, U.S.A.

10. *Peter Altenberg.* 1909.
Oil on canvas, 29⅞×28 in. (76×71 cm).
Private Collection.

11. *Hans Tietze and Erica Tietze-Conrat*. 1909.
    Oil on canvas, 30 ⅛ × 53 ⅝ in. (76.5 × 136.2 cm).
    The Museum of Modern Art, New York.
    Abby Aldrich Rockefeller Fund.

12. *'Les Dents du Midi'*. 1910.
    Oil on canvas, 31 ¼ × 45 ½ in. (79.5 × 115.5 cm).
    Private Collection, Switzerland.

11

12

13. *Bessie Bruce*. 1910.
    Oil on canvas, 28 ³/₈ × 35 ⁷/₈ in. (72 × 91 cm).
    Staatliche Museen Preussischer Kulturbesitz, Nationalgalerie, Berlin.

13

14. *Joseph de Montesquiou-Fezensac.* 1910.
Oil on canvas, 31 ½ × 24 ¾ in. (80 × 63 cm).
Moderna Museet, Stockholm.

15. *Victoria de Montesquiou-Fezensac.* 1910.
Oil on canvas, 37 ¼ × 19 ¼ in. (94.6 × 48.9 cm).
Cincinnati Art Museum.

16. *Conte Verona*. 1910.
   Oil on canvas, 27 ¾ × 23 ⅛ in. (70.6 × 58.7 cm).
   Private Collection, U.S.A.

17. *Herwarth Walden*. 1910.
     Oil on canvas, 39 ⅜ × 27 ¼ in. (100 × 69.3 cm).
     Staatsgalerie Stuttgart.

17

18. *Paul Scheerbart.* 1910.
    Oil on canvas, 27⅝ × 18½ in. (70 × 47 cm).
    Private Collection, U.S.A.

19. *Egon Wellesz*. 1911.
Oil on canvas, 29¾ × 27⅛ in. (75.5 × 68.9 cm).
Hirshhorn Museum and Sculpture Garden,
Smithsonian Institution, Washington, D.C.

19

20. *Else Kupfer*. 1911.
    Oil on canvas, 35 ½ × 28 ⅛ in. (90 × 71.5 cm).
    Kunsthaus, Zurich.

21. *Baron Viktor von Dirsztay.* 1911.
    Oil on canvas, 38 ¾ × 28 ¾ in. (98.5 × 73 cm).
    Sprengel Museum, Hannover.

22. *Portrait of a Boy, Jacques de Menasce.* 1911.
    Oil on canvas, 37 3/8 × 18 1/2 in. (95 × 47 cm).
    Staatliche Museen Preussischer Kulturbesitz, Nationalgalerie, Berlin.

23. *The Annunciation.* 1911.
    Oil on canvas, 32 5/8 × 48 1/4 in. (83 × 122.5 cm).
    Museum am Ostwall, Dortmund.

24. *Alpine Landscape, Mürren.* 1912.
    Oil on canvas, 27 3/4 × 37 5/8 in. (70.5 × 95.5 cm).
    Bayerische Staatsgemäldesammlungen, Munich.

22

23

24

25. *Double Portrait (Kokoschka and Alma Mahler).* 1912–13.
Oil on canvas, 39 ⅜ × 35 ½ in. (100 × 90 cm).
Museum Folkwang, Essen.

26. *Alma Mahler*. 1912.
   Oil on canvas, 24 3/8 × 22 in. (62 × 56 cm).
   The National Museum of Modern Art, Tokyo.

27. *Self-portrait.* 1913.
    Oil on canvas, 32 ⅛ × 19 ½ in. (81.6 × 49.5 cm).
    The Museum of Modern Art, New York. Purchase.

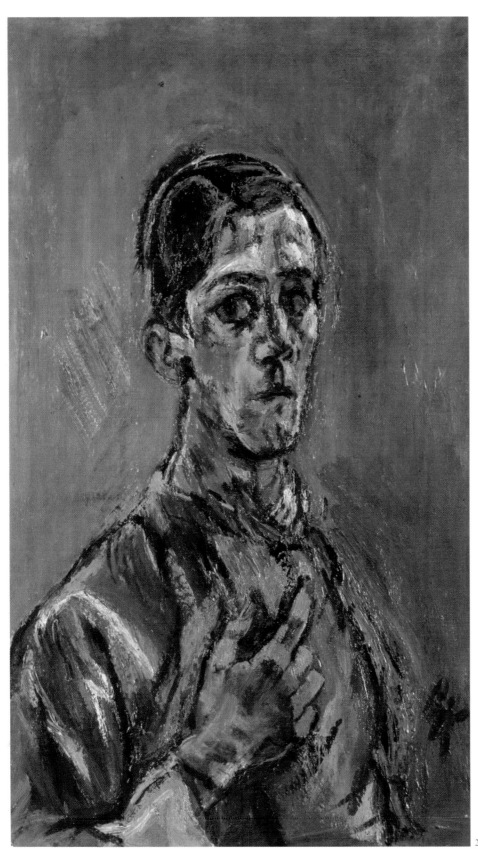

28. *Two Nudes (the Lovers).* 1913.
Oil on canvas, 64⅛×38⅜ in. (163×97.5 cm).
Museum of Fine Arts, Boston.

29. *Franz Hauer.* 1913.
    Oil on canvas, 47¼ × 41¾ in. (120 × 106 cm).
    Museum of Art, Rhode Island School of Design, Providence.

30. *The Tempest.* 1913.
   Oil on canvas, 71 ¼ × 87 in. (181 × 221 cm).
   Kunstmuseum, Basel.

30

31. *Still-life with Putto and Rabbit.* 1913–14.
Oil on canvas, 35½ × 47¼ in. (90 × 120 cm).
Kunsthaus, Zurich.

32. *Knight Errant.* 1915.
Oil on canvas, 35¼ × 70⅞ in. (89.5 × 180.1 cm).
Solomon R. Guggenheim Museum, New York.

31

32

33. *Woman with Parrot.* 1916.
    Oil on canvas, $33\frac{1}{8} \times 20\frac{1}{8}$ in. $(84 \times 51$ cm).
    Staatsgalerie, Stuttgart.

34. *Lovers with Cat*. 1917.
    Oil on canvas, 36⅞ × 51⅜ in. (93.5 × 130.5 cm).
    Kunsthaus, Zurich.

34

35. *The Friends*. 1917–18.
   Oil on canvas, 40⅛ × 59½ in. (102 × 151 cm).
   Neue Galerie der Stadt Linz, Wolfgang-Gurlitt-Museum.

35

36. *Self-portrait (Hand Touching Face).* 1918–19.
Oil on canvas, 32 ⅞ × 24 ¾ in. (83.6 × 62.8 cm).
Leopold Collection, Vienna.

37. *The Power of Music.* 1920.
Oil on canvas, 39 ⅜ × 59 ⅝ in. (100 × 151.5 cm).
Stedelijk van Abbemuseum, Eindhoven.

38. *Woman in Blue.* 1919.
Oil on canvas, 29 ½ × 39 ⅜ in. (75 × 100 cm).
Staatsgalerie, Stuttgart.

39. *Self-portrait with Doll.* 1922.
Oil on canvas, 31 ½ × 47 ¼ in. (80 × 120 cm).
Staatliche Museen Preussischer Kulturbesitz, Nationalgalerie, Berlin.

36

37

38

40. *Dresden, Neustadt II*. 1921.
   Oil on canvas, 23 ½ × 31 ½ in. (59.7 × 80 cm).
   Detroit Institute of Arts.

40

41. *Two Girls*. 1921–22.
Oil on canvas, 46⅛×31½ in. (117×80 cm).
Private Collection, U.S.A.

42. *Mother and Child (embracing)*. 1921–22.
Oil on canvas, 47 5/8 × 31 7/8 in. (121 × 81 cm).
Österreichische Galerie, Vienna.

43. *Girl with Doll.* 1921–22.
Oil on canvas, 36 × 32 in. (91.5 × 81.2 cm).
Detroit Institute of Arts.

44. *Dresden, Neustadt VII.* 1922.
Oil on canvas, 31½ × 47¼ in. (80 × 120 cm).
Kunsthalle, Hamburg.

44

45. *Dresden, Augustus Bridge with Steamer II*. 1923.
Oil on canvas, 25⅝ × 37⅝ in. (65 × 95.5 cm).
Stedelijk Van Abbe Museum, Eindhoven.

46. *Dresden, the Elbe Bridges (with Figure from Behind)*. 1923.
Oil on canvas, 25¾ × 37⅝ in. (65.5 × 95.7 cm).
Museum Folkwang, Essen.

47. *The Slave Girl*. 1921.
     Oil on canvas, 43 ½ × 31 ½ in. (110.5 × 80 cm).
     Saint Louis Art Museum.

48. *Self-portrait with Crossed Arms.* 1923.
Oil on canvas, 43 ¼ × 27 ⅝ in. (110 × 70 cm).
Private Collection.

49. *Arnold Schoenberg*. 1924.
Oil on canvas, 37¾×29⅛ in. (96×74 cm).
Private Collection, U.S.A.

50. *Nancy Cunard.* 1924.
    Oil on canvas, 45 $\frac{5}{8}$ × 28 $\frac{3}{4}$ in. (116 × 73 cm).
    Sprengel Museum, Hannover.

51. *London, Waterloo Bridge.* 1926.
Oil on canvas, 35 × 51 ¼ in. (89 × 130 cm).
National Museum of Wales, Cardiff.

52. *Karl Kraus II.* 1925.
Oil on canvas, 25 ⅝ × 39 ⅜ in. (65 × 100 cm).
Museum Moderner Kunst, Vienna.

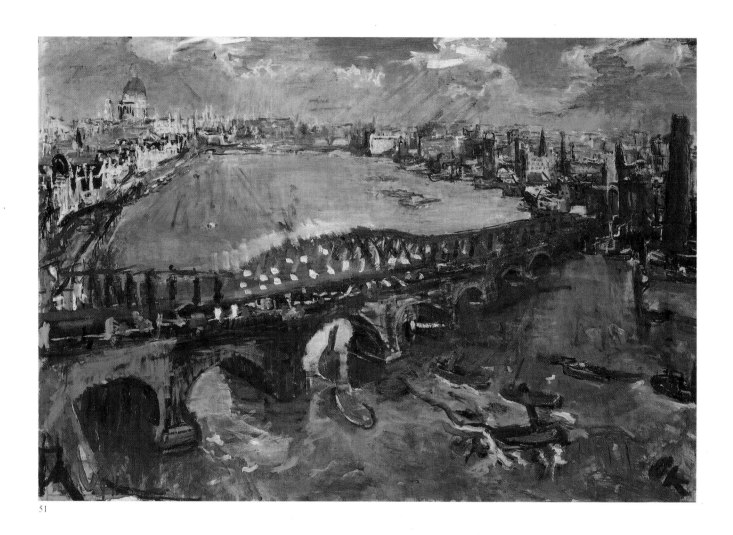

51

52

53. *London, Large Thames View I.* 1926.
   Oil on canvas, 35 ½ × 51 ¼ in. (90 × 130 cm).
   Albright-Knox Art Gallery, Buffalo, New York.

54. *Leo Kestenberg*. 1926–27.
Oil on canvas, 50 × 40⅛ in. (127 × 102 cm).
Ruth Gladstein and Rachel Epstein Collection, Haifa.

55. *Adèle Astaire.* 1926.
   Oil on canvas, 38 ¼ × 51 ⅜ in. (97 × 130.5 cm).
   Kunsthaus, Zurich.

55

56. *Mandrill.* 1926.
Oil on canvas, 50 ¼ × 40 ¼ in. (127.5 × 102.3 cm).
Museum Boymans-van Beuningen, Rotterdam.

57. *Tigon.* 1926.
Oil on canvas, 37 ¾ × 50 ¾ in. (96 × 129 cm).
Österreichische Galerie, Vienna.

58. *Lyon.* 1927.
Oil on canvas, $38\,^3/_8 \times 51\,^1/_4$ in. (97.1 × 130.2 cm).
Phillips Collection, Washington, D.C.

58

59. *Marczell von Nemeš.* 1928.
Oil on canvas, 53 ⅛ × 37 ¾ in. (135 × 96 cm).
Neue Galerie de Stadt Linz, Wolfgang-Gurlitt-Museum.

60. *The Marabout of Temacine (Sidi Ahmet Ben Tidjani).* 1928.
   Oil on canvas, 38 ³/₄ × 51 ³/₈ in. (98.5 × 130.5 cm).
   Private Collection.

60

61. *Jerusalem.* 1929.
Oil on canvas, 31½×50¾ in. (80×129 cm).
Detroit Institute of Arts.

62. *Arab Women and Child.* 1929.
Oil on canvas, 34⅞×50⅜ in. (88.5×128 cm).
Private Collection
(on loan to the Tate Gallery).

61

62

63. *Vienna, View from the Wilhelminenberg.* 1931.
   Oil on canvas, 36 ¼ × 52 ¾ in. (92 × 134 cm).
   Historisches Museum, Vienna.

63

64. *Pan (Trudl with Goat)*. 1931.
Oil on canvas, 34¼×51¼ in. (87×130 cm).
Sprengel Museum, Hannover.

65. *Mother and Child (Trudl with Noh Mask)*. 1934.
Oil on canvas, 22×29½ in. (56×75 cm).
Galerie Würthle, Vienna.

64

65

66. *Prague, View from the Villa Kramář.* 1934–35.
Oil on canvas, 35 ½ × 47 ⅝ in. (90 × 121 cm).
Národní Galerie, Prague.

67. *Thomas G. Masaryk.* 1936.
Oil on canvas, 38 ⅜ × 51 ⅝ in. (97.7 × 131 cm).
Museum of Art, Carnegie Institute, Pittsburgh.

66

67

68. *Prague, View from the Moldau Pier towards the Kleinseite and Hradschin IV.* 1936.
   Oil on canvas, 38 ⅝ × 51 ¼ in. (98 × 130 cm).
   Phillips Collection, Washington, D.C.

68

69. *Nymph.* 1936.
    Oil on canvas, 37⅜ × 29⅞ in. (95 × 76 cm).
    Národní Galerie, Prague.

70. *Olda Palkovská*. 1937.
    Oil on canvas, 35 ½ × 26 ⅜ in. (90 × 67 cm).
    Private Collection.

71. *Self-portrait of a "Degenerate Artist"* 1937.
Oil on canvas, 43 ¼ × 33 ½ in. (110 × 85 cm).
Private Collection (on loan to the Scottish National Gallery of Modern Art).

72. *Prague, Nostalgia.* 1938.
    Oil on canvas, $22 \times 29\,^7/_8$ in. (56×76 cm).
    Lord Croft (on loan to the Scottish National Gallery of Modern Art).

73. *Polperro II.* 1939.
    Oil on canvas, $23\,^7/_8 \times 33\,^7/_8$ in. (60.5×86 cm).
    Tate Gallery, London.

74. *Michael Croft*. 1938–39.
Oil on canvas, 30 × 25 ⅛ in. (76.2 × 63.7 cm).
Lord Croft (on loan to the Scottish National Gallery of Modern Art).

75. *Posy Croft*. 1939.
   Oil on canvas, $30 \times 24\,7/8$ in. (76.2×63.5 cm).
   Private Collection (on loan to the Scottish National Gallery of Modern Art).

76

77

76. *The Crab.* 1939–40.
    Oil on canvas, 25 × 30 in. (63.4 × 76.2 cm).
    Tate Gallery, London.

77. *Summer II (Zrání).* 1939–40.
    Oil on canvas, 26⅞ × 32⅝ in. (68.3 × 82.9 cm).
    Scottish National Gallery of Modern Art, Edinburgh.

78. *The Red Egg.* 1940–41.
    Oil on canvas, 24¾ × 29⅞ in. (63 × 76 cm).
    Národní Galerie, Prague.

78

79. *Anschluß—Alice in Wonderland.* 1942.
Oil on canvas, 24⅞ × 29 in. (63.5 × 73.6 cm).
Wiener Städtische Wechselseitige Versicherungsanstalt (on loan to the Historisches
Museum, Vienna).

80. *Loreley*. 1941–42.
    Oil on canvas, 24⅞×30⅛ in. (63.5×76.4 cm).
    Tate Gallery, London.

80

81

81. *Marianne-Maquis*. 1942.
Oil on canvas, 24⁷⁄₈ × 29⁷⁄₈ in. (63.5 × 76 cm).
Tate Gallery, London.

82. *'What We Are Fighting For'*. 1943.
Oil on canvas, 45⁷⁄₈ × 59⁷⁄₈ in. (116.5 × 152 cm).
Kunsthaus, Zurich.

83. *Ivan Maisky*. 1942–43.
Oil on canvas, 40¹⁄₈ × 30³⁄₈ in. (102 × 77 cm).
Tate Gallery, London.

82

84. *Minona.* 1944–45.
   Oil on canvas, 20 × 24 in. (50.8 × 61 cm).
   Fondation à la Memoire d'Oskar Kokoschka, Musée Jenisch, Vevey.

84

85. *Kathleen, Countess of Drogheda.* 1946.
Oil on canvas, 40⅛ × 29⅞ in. (102 × 76 cm).
Private Collection.

86. *Montana.* 1947.
Oil on canvas, 35 ½ × 47 ¼ in. (90 × 120 cm).
Kunsthaus, Zurich.

87. *Self-portrait (Fiesole)*. 1948.
  Oil on canvas, 25¾×21⅝ in. (65.5×55 cm).
  Fondation à la Memoire d'Oskar Kokoschka, Musée Jenisch, Vevey.

88. *Cardinal dalla Costa.* 1948.
Oil on canvas, 38⅜×28⅛ in. (97.5×71.5 cm).
Phillips Collection, Washington, D.C.

89. *Florence, View from the Torre Antinori.* 1948.
    Oil on canvas, 33 ½ × 43 ¼ in. (85 × 110 cm).
    Private Collection.

90. *Theodor Körner.* 1949.
   Oil on canvas, 39⅜ × 31⅞ in. (100 × 81 cm).
   Neue Galerie der Stadt Linz, Wolfgang-Gurlitt-Museum.

91. *Louis Krohnberg.* 1950.
   Oil on canvas, $39\frac{3}{8} \times 29\frac{1}{2}$ in. (100×75 cm).
   Private Collection.

93. *Pablo Casals.* 1954.
Oil on canvas, 33 ½ × 25 ⅝ in. (85 × 65 cm).
Private Collection.

94. *London, Chelsea Reach.* 1957.
    Oil on canvas, 29 ½ × 39 ¾ in. (75 × 101 cm).
    Private Collection.

95. *Lake Geneva with Steamer.* 1957.
    Oil on canvas, 31 ⅞ × 45 ⅝ in. (81 × 116 cm).
    Fondation à la Memoire d'Oskar Kokoschka, Musée Jenisch, Vevey.

94

95

96. *London, View of the Thames from Shell-Mex House.* 1959.
Oil on canvas, 36 × 48 ⅜ in. (91.5 × 123 cm).
Tate Gallery, London.

96

97. *Herodotus.* 1960–64.
   Oil on canvas, $70^7/_8 \times 47^1/_4$ in. (180 × 120 cm).
   Österreichische Galerie, Vienna.

98. *Self-portrait with Olda.* 1966.
Oil on canvas, 35 × 45 ⁵⁄₈ in. (89 × 116 cm).
Landessammlungen Rupertinum, Salzburg.

99. *New York, Manhattan with the Empire State Building.* 1966.
Oil on canvas, 40 × 54 in. (101.5 × 137 cm).
Private Collection.

100. *Saul and David.* 1966.
Oil on canvas, 39 ³⁄₈ × 51 ¼ in. (100 × 130 cm).
Tel Aviv Museum of Art.

98

99

100

101. *Morning and Evening (The Power of Music II).* 1966.
Oil on canvas, 39 $^5/_8$ × 51 $^1/_4$ in. (100 × 130 cm).
Kunsthaus, Zurich.

101

102. Self-portrait. 1969.
    Oil on canvas, 35 5/8 × 27 3/4 in. (90.5 × 70.4 cm).
    Private Collection (on loan to the Tate Gallery).

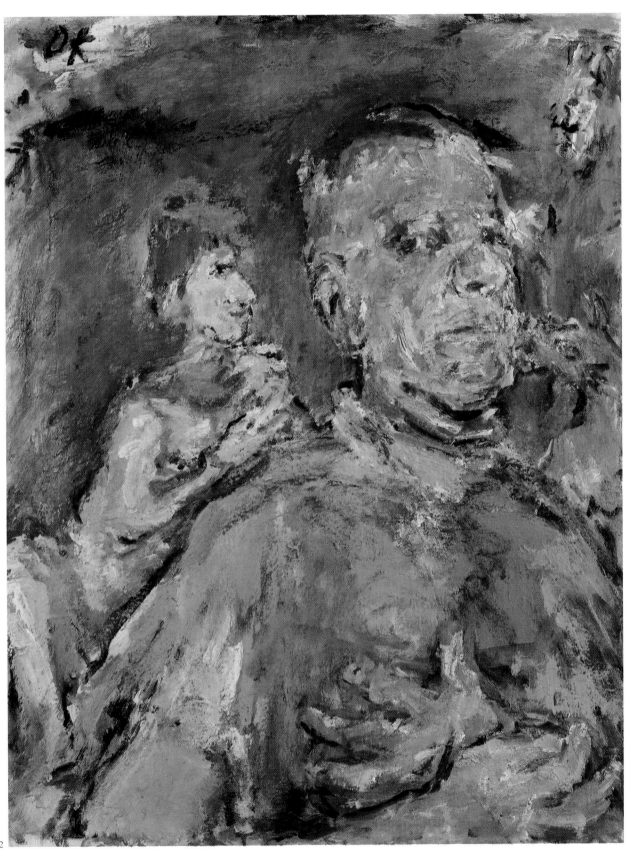

103. *View of London with St. Paul's.* 1970.
Oil on canvas, 39¾ × 54 in. (101 × 137 cm).
Private Collection.

104. *The Duke and Duchess of Hamilton.* 1969.
Oil on canvas, 35⅜ × 51⅛ in. (89.8 × 129.8 cm).
Scottish National Portrait Gallery, Edinburgh.

103

104

105. *Time, Gentlemen Please.* 1971–72.
Oil on canvas, 51 ¼ × 39 ⅜ in. (130 × 100 cm).
Tate Gallery, London.

106. *Peer Gynt*. 1973.
Oil on canvas, 45¼×35 in. (115×89 cm).
Private Collection.

107. *Theseus and Antiope.* 1958/75.
Oil on canvas, 76$\frac{3}{4}$ × 65 in. (195 × 165 cm).
Fondation à la Memoire d'Oskar Kokoschka, Musée Jenisch, Vevey.

LIST OF ILLUSTRATIONS

1. *Still-life with Pineapple.* 1909.
Oil on canvas, 42⅞×30¾ in.
(109×78 cm).
Staatliche Museen Preussischer
Kulturbesitz, Nationalgalerie, Berlin.

2. *Father Hirsch.* 1909.
Oil on canvas, 27¾×24⅝ in.
(70.5×62.5 cm).
Neue Galerie der Stadt Linz, Wolfgang-
Gurlitt-Museum.

3. *Martha Hirsch.* 1909.
Oil on canvas, 34⅝×27⅝ in.
(88×70 cm).
Private Collection, U.S.A.

4. *Child with the Hands of its Father and
Mother.* 1909.
Oil on canvas, 28⅜×20½ in.
(72×52 cm).
Österreichische Galerie, Vienna.

5. *Children Playing.* 1909.
Oil on canvas, 28⅜×42½ in.
(72×108 cm).
Wilhelm Lehmbruck Museum,
Duisburg.

6. *Lotte Franzos.* 1909.
Oil on canvas, 45¼×31¼ in.
(115×79.5 cm).
Phillips Collection, Washington, D.C.

7. *Felix Albrecht Harta.* 1909.
Oil on canvas, 28¾×20⅝ in.
(73.1×52.5 cm).
Hirshhorn Museum and Sculpture
Garden, Smithsonian Institution,
Washington, D.C.

8. *Adolf Loos.* 1909.
Oil on canvas, 29⅛×35⅞ in.
(74×91 cm).
Staatliche Museen Preussischer
Kulturbesitz, Nationalgalerie, Berlin.

9. *Ludwig Ritter von Janikowski.* 1909.
Oil on canvas, 23¾×22½ in.
(60.2×57.2 cm).
Private Collection, U.S.A.

10. *Peter Altenberg.* 1909.
Oil on canvas, 29⅞×28 in. (76×71 cm).
Private Collection.

11. *Hans Tietze and Erica Tietze-Conrat.*
1909.
Oil on canvas, 30⅛×53⅝ in.
(76.5×136.2 cm).
The Museum of Modern Art,
New York. Abby Aldrich Rockefeller
Fund.

12. *'Les Dents du Midi'.* 1910.
Oil on canvas, 31¼×45½ in.
(79.5×115.5 cm).
Private Collection, Switzerland.

13. *Bessie Bruce.* 1910.
Oil on canvas, 28⅜×35⅞ in.
(72×91 cm).
Staatliche Museen Preussischer
Kulturbesitz, Nationalgalerie, Berlin.

14. *Joseph de Montesquiou-Fezensac.* 1910.
Oil on canvas, 31½×24¾ in.
(80×63 cm).
Moderna Museet, Stockholm.

15. *Victoria de Montesquiou-Fezensac.* 1910.
Oil on canvas, 37¼×19¼ in.
(94.6×48.9 cm).
Cincinnati Art Museum.

16. *Conte Verona.* 1910.
Oil on canvas, 27¾×23⅛ in.
(70.6×58.7 cm).
Private Collection, U.S.A.

17. *Herwarth Walden.* 1910.
Oil on canvas, 39⅜×27¼ in.
(100×69.3 cm).
Staatsgalerie Stuttgart.

18. *Paul Scheerbart.* 1910.
Oil on canvas, 27⅝×18½ in.
(70×47 cm).
Private Collection, U.S.A.

19. *Egon Wellesz.* 1911.
Oil on canvas, 29¾×27⅛ in.
(75.5×68.9 cm).
Hirshhorn Museum and Sculpture
Garden, Smithsonian Institution,
Washington, D.C.

20. *Else Kupfer.* 1911.
Oil on canvas, 35½×28⅛ in.
(90×71.5 cm).
Kunsthaus, Zurich.

21. *Baron Viktor von Dirsztay.* 1911.
Oil on canvas, 38¾×28¾ in.
(98.5×73 cm).
Sprengel Museum, Hannover.

22. *Portrait of a Boy, Jacques de Menasce.*
1911.
Oil on canvas, 37⅜×18½ in.
(95×47 cm).
Staatliche Museen Preussischer
Kulturbesitz, Nationalgalerie, Berlin.

23. *The Annunciation.* 1911.
Oil on canvas, 32⅝×48¼ in.
(83×122.5 cm).
Museum am Ostwall, Dortmund.

24. *Alpine Landscape, Mürren.* 1912.
Oil on canvas, 27¾×37⅝ in.
(70.5×95.5 cm).
Bayerische Staatsgemäldesammlungen,
Munich.

25. *Double Portrait (Kokoschka and Alma
Mahler).* 1912–13.
Oil on canvas, 39⅜×35½ in.
(100×90 cm).
Museum Folkwang, Essen.

26. *Alma Mahler.* 1912.
Oil on canvas, 24⅜×22 in. (62×56 cm).
The National Museum of Modern Art,
Tokyo.

27. *Self-portrait.* 1913.
Oil on canvas, 32⅛×19½ in.
(81.6×49.5 cm).
The Museum of Modern Art, New
York. Purchase.

28. *Two Nudes (the Lovers).* 1913.
Oil on canvas, 64⅛×38⅜ in.
(163×97.5 cm).
Museum of Fine Arts, Boston.

29. *Franz Hauer.* 1913.
Oil on canvas, 47¼×41¾ in.
(120×106 cm).
Museum of Art, Rhode Island School
of Design, Providence.

30. *The Tempest.* 1913.
Oil on canvas, 71¼×87 in.
(181×221 cm).
Kunstmuseum, Basel.

31. *Still-life with Putto and Rabbit.* 1913–14.
Oil on canvas, 35½×47¼ in.
(90×120 cm).
Kunsthaus, Zurich.

32. *Knight Errant.* 1915.
Oil on canvas, 35¼×70⅞ in.
(89.5×180.1 cm).
Solomon R. Guggenheim Museum, New
York.

33. *Woman with Parrot.* 1916.
Oil on canvas, 33⅛×20⅛ in.
(84×51 cm).
Staatsgalerie, Stuttgart.

34. *Lovers with Cat.* 1917.
Oil on canvas, 36⅞×51⅜ in.
(93.5×130.5 cm).
Kunsthaus, Zurich.

35. *The Friends.* 1917–18.
Oil on canvas, 40⅛×59½ in.
(102×151 cm).
Neue Galerie der Stadt Linz, Wolfgang-
Gurlitt-Museum.

36. *Self-portrait (Hand Touching Face).*
1918–19.
Oil on canvas, 32⅞×24¾ in.
(83.6×62.8 cm).
Leopold Collection, Vienna.

37. *The Power of Music.* 1920.
Oil on canvas, 39⅜×59⅝ in.
(100×151.5 cm).
Stedelijk van Abbemuseum, Eindhoven.

38. *Woman in Blue.* 1919.
Oil on canvas, 29½×39⅜ in.
(75×100 cm).
Staatsgalerie, Stuttgart.

39. *Self-portrait with Doll.* 1922.
Oil on canvas, 31½×47¼ in.
(80×120 cm).
Staatliche Museen Preussischer
Kulturbesitz, Nationalgalerie, Berlin.

40. *Dresden, Neustadt II.* 1921.
Oil on canvas, 23½×31½ in.
(59.7×80 cm).
Detroit Institute of Arts.

41. *Two Girls.* 1921–22.
Oil on canvas, 46⅛×31½ in.
(117×80 cm).
Private Collection, U.S.A.

42. *Mother and Child (embracing)*. 1921–22.
Oil on canvas, 47⅝ × 31⅞ in.
(121 × 81 cm).
Österreichische Galerie, Vienna.

43. *Girl with Doll*. 1921–22.
Oil on canvas, 36 × 32 in.
(91.5 × 81.2 cm).
Detroit Institute of Arts.

44. *Dresden, Neustadt VII*. 1922.
Oil on canvas, 31½ × 47¼ in.
(80 × 120 cm).
Kunsthalle, Hamburg.

45. *Dresden, Augustus Bridge with Steamer II*. 1923.
Oil on canvas, 25⅝ × 37⅝ in.
(65 × 95.5 cm).
Stedelijk Van Abbe Museum, Eindhoven.

46. *Dresden, the Elbe Bridges (with Figure from Behind)*. 1923.
Oil on canvas, 25¾ × 37⅝ in.
(65.5 × 95.7 cm).
Museum Folkwang, Essen.

47. *The Slave Girl*. 1921.
Oil on canvas, 43½ × 31½ in.
(110.5 × 80 cm).
Saint Louis Art Museum.

48. *Self-portrait with Crossed Arms*. 1923.
Oil on canvas, 43¼ × 27⅝ in.
(110 × 70 cm).
Private Collection.

49. *Arnold Schoenberg*. 1924.
Oil on canvas, 37¾ × 29⅛ in.
(96 × 74 cm).
Private Collection, U.S.A.

50. *Nancy Cunard*. 1924.
Oil on canvas, 45⅝ × 28¾ in.
(116 × 73 cm).
Sprengel Museum, Hannover.

51. *London, Waterloo Bridge*. 1926.
Oil on canvas, 35 × 51¼ in.
(89 × 130 cm).
National Museum of Wales, Cardiff.

52. *Karl Kraus II*. 1925.
Oil on canvas, 25⅝ × 39⅜ in.
(65 × 100 cm).
Museum Moderner Kunst, Vienna.

53. *London, Large Thames View I*. 1926.
Oil on canvas, 35½ × 51¼ in.
(90 × 130 cm).
Albright-Knox Art Gallery, Buffalo, New York.

54. *Leo Kestenberg*. 1926–27.
Oil on canvas, 50 × 40⅛ in.
(127 × 102 cm).
Ruth Gladstein and Rachel Epstein Collection, Haifa.

55. *Adèle Astaire*. 1926.
Oil on canvas, 38¼ × 51⅜ in.
(97 × 130.5 cm).
Kunsthaus, Zurich.

56. *Mandrill*. 1926.
Oil on canvas, 50¼ × 40¼ in.
(127.5 × 102.3 cm).
Museum Boymans-van Beuningen, Rotterdam.

57. *Tigon*. 1926.
Oil on canvas, 37¾ × 50¾ in.
(96 × 129 cm).
Österreichische Galerie, Vienna.

58. *Lyon*. 1927.
Oil on canvas, 38⅜ × 51¼ in.
(97.1 × 130.2 cm).
Phillips Collection, Washington, D.C.

59. *Marczell von Nemeš*. 1928.
Oil on canvas, 53⅛ × 37¾ in.
(135 × 96 cm).
Neue Galerie de Stadt Linz, Wolfgang-Gurlitt-Museum.

60. *The Marabout of Temacine (Sidi Ahmet Ben Tidjani)*. 1928.
Oil on canvas, 38¾ × 51⅜ in.
(98.5 × 130.5 cm).
Private Collection.

61. *Jerusalem*. 1929.
Oil on canvas, 31½ × 50¾ in.
(80 × 129 cm).
Detroit Institute of Arts.

62. *Arab Women and Child*. 1929.
Oil on canvas, 34⅞ × 50⅜ in.
(88.5 × 128 cm).
Private Collection
(on loan to the Tate Gallery).

63. *Vienna, View from the Wilhelminenberg*. 1931.
Oil on canvas, 36¼ × 52¾ in.
(92 × 134 cm).
Historisches Museum, Vienna.

64. *Pan (Trudl with Goat)*. 1931.
Oil on canvas, 34¼ × 51¼ in.
(87 × 130 cm).
Sprengel Museum, Hannover.

65. *Mother and Child (Trudl with Noh Mask)*. 1934.
Oil on canvas, 22 × 29½ in. (56 × 75 cm).
Galerie Würthle, Vienna.

66. *Prague, View from the Villa Kramář*. 1934–35.
Oil on canvas, 35½ × 47⅝ in.
(90 × 121 cm).
Národní Galerie, Prague.

67. *Thomas G. Masaryk*. 1936.
Oil on canvas, 38⅜ × 51⅝ in.
(97.7 × 131 cm).
Museum of Art, Carnegie Institute, Pittsburgh.

68. *Prague, View from the Moldau Pier towards the Kleinseite and Hradschin IV*. 1936.
Oil on canvas, 38⅝ × 51¼ in.
(98 × 130 cm).
Phillips Collection, Washington, D.C.

69. *Nymph*. 1936.
Oil on canvas, 37⅜ × 29⅞ in.
(95 × 76 cm).
Národní Galerie, Prague.

70. *Olda Palkovská*. 1937.
Oil on canvas, 35½ × 26⅜ in.
(90 × 67 cm).
Private Collection.

71. *Self-portrait of a "Degenerate Artist"* 1937.
Oil on canvas, 43¼ × 33½ in.
(110 × 85 cm).
Private Collection (on loan to the Scottish National Gallery of Modern Art).

72. *Prague, Nostalgia*. 1938.
Oil on canvas, 22 × 29⅞ in.
(56 × 76 cm).
Lord Croft (on loan to the Scottish National Gallery of Modern Art).

73. *Polperro II*. 1939.
Oil on canvas, 23⅞ × 33⅞ in.
(60.5 × 86 cm).
Tate Gallery, London.

74. *Michael Croft*. 1938–39.
Oil on canvas, 30 × 25⅛ in.
(76.2 × 63.7 cm).
Lord Croft (on loan to the Scottish National Gallery of Modern Art).

75. *Posy Croft*. 1939.
Oil on canvas, 30 × 24⅞ in.
(76.2 × 63.5 cm).
Private Collection (on loan to the Scottish National Gallery of Modern Art).

76. *The Crab*. 1939–40.
Oil on canvas, 25 × 30 in.
(63.4 × 76.2 cm).
Tate Gallery, London.

77. *Summer II (Zrání)*. 1939–40.
Oil on canvas, 26⅞ × 32⅝ in.
(68.3 × 82.9 cm).
Scottish National Gallery of Modern Art, Edinburgh.

78. *The Red Egg*. 1940–41.
Oil on canvas, 24¾ × 29⅞ in.
(63 × 76 cm).
Národní Galerie, Prague.

79. *Anschluß—Alice in Wonderland*. 1942.
Oil on canvas, 24⅞ × 29 in.
(63.5 × 73.6 cm).
Wiener Städtische Wechselseitige Versicherungsanstalt (on loan to the Historisches Museum, Vienna).

80. *Loreley*. 1941–42.
Oil on canvas, 24⅞ × 30⅛ in.
(63.5 × 76.4 cm).
Tate Gallery, London.

81. *Marianne-Maquis*. 1942.
Oil on canvas, 24⅞ × 29⅞ in.
(63.5 × 76 cm).
Tate Gallery, London.

82. *'What We Are Fighting For'.* 1943.
Oil on canvas, 45⅞ × 59⅞ in.
(116.5 × 152 cm).
Kunsthaus, Zurich.

83. *Ivan Maisky.* 1942–43.
Oil on canvas, 40⅛ × 30⅜ in.
(102 × 77 cm).
Tate Gallery, London.

84. *Minona.* 1944–45.
Oil on canvas, 20 × 24 in. (50.8 × 61 cm).
Fondation à la Memoire d'Oskar
Kokoschka, Musée Jenisch, Vevey.

85. *Kathleen, Countess of Drogheda.* 1946.
Oil on canvas, 40⅛ × 29⅞ in.
(102 × 76 cm).
Private Collection.

86. *Montana.* 1947.
Oil on canvas, 35½ × 47¼ in.
(90 × 120 cm).
Kunsthaus, Zurich.

87. *Self-portrait (Fiesole).* 1948.
Oil on canvas, 25¾ × 21⅝ in.
(65.5 × 55 cm).
Fondation à la Memoire d'Oskar
Kokoschka, Musée Jenisch, Vevey..

88. *Cardinal dalla Costa.* 1948.
Oil on canvas, 38⅜ × 28⅛ in.
(97.5 × 71.5 cm).
Phillips Collection, Washington, D.C.

89. *Florence, View from the Torre
Antinori.* 1948.
Oil on canvas, 33½ × 43¼ in.
(85 × 110 cm).
Private Collection.

90. *Theodor Körner.* 1949.
Oil on canvas, 39⅜ × 31⅞ in.
(100 × 81 cm).
Neue Galerie der Stadt Linz, Wolfgang-
Gurlitt-Museum.

91. *Louis Krohnberg.* 1950.
Oil on canvas, 39⅜ × 29½ in.
(100 × 75 cm).
Private Collection.

92. *The Prometheus Saga.* 1950.
Tempera on three canvases,
90½ × 90½ in.; 90½ × 137¾ in.;
90½ × 90½ in.
(230 × 230 cm; 230 × 350 cm;
230 × 230 cm).
Courtauld Institute Galleries, Princes
Gate Collection, London.

93. *Pablo Casals.* 1954.
Oil on canvas, 33½ × 25⅝ in.
(85 × 65 cm).
Private Collection.

94. *London, Chelsea Reach.* 1957.
Oil on canvas, 29½ × 39¾ in.
(75 × 101 cm).
Private Collection.

95. *Lake Geneva with Steamer.* 1957.
Oil on canvas, 31⅞ × 45⅝ in.
(81 × 116 cm).
Fondation à la Memoire d'Oskar
Kokoschka, Musée Jenisch, Vevey.

96. *London, View of the Thames from
Shell-Mex House.* 1959.
Oil on canvas, 36 × 48⅜ in.
(91.5 × 123 cm).
Tate Gallery, London.

97. *Herodotus.* 1960–64.
Oil on canvas, 70⅞ × 47¼ in.
(180 × 120 cm).
Österreichische Galerie, Vienna.

98. *Self-portrait with Olda.* 1966.
Oil on canvas, 35 × 45⅝ in.
(89 × 116 cm).
Landessammlungen Rupertinum,
Salzburg.

99. *New York, Manhattan with the
Empire State Building.* 1966.
Oil on canvas, 40 × 54 in.
(101.5 × 137 cm).
Private Collection.

100. *Saul and David.* 1966.
Oil on canvas, 39⅜ × 51¼ in.
(100 × 130 cm).
Tel Aviv Museum of Art.

101. *Morning and Evening (The Power of
Music II).* 1966.
Oil on canvas, 39⅝ × 51¼ in.
(100 × 130 cm).
Kunsthaus, Zurich.

102. Self-portrait. 1969.
Oil on canvas, 35⅝ × 27¾ in.
(90.5 × 70.4 cm).
Private Collection (on loan to the Tate
Gallery).

103. *View of London with St. Paul's.* 1970.
Oil on canvas, 39¾ × 54 in.
(101 × 137 cm).
Private Collection.

104. *The Duke and Duchess of Hamilton.* 1969.
Oil on canvas, 35⅜ × 51⅛ in.
(89.8 × 129.8 cm).
Scottish National Portrait Gallery,
Edinburgh.

105. *Time, Gentlemen Please.* 1971–72.
Oil on canvas, 51¼ × 39⅜ in.
(130 × 100 cm).
Tate Gallery, London.

106. *Peer Gynt.* 1973.
Oil on canvas, 45¼ × 35 in. (115 × 89 cm).
Private Collection.

107. *Theseus and Antiope.* 1958/75.
Oil on canvas, 76¾ × 65 in.
(195 × 165 cm).
Fondation à la Memoire d'Oskar
Kokoschka, Musée Jenisch, Vevey.